CU00481567

ISRAELI PEACE / PALESTINIAN JUSTICE

Liberation Theology and the Peace Process

Thomas L. Are

CLARITY

In-house editor: Diana G. Collier

Cataloging in Publication Data:

Are, Thomas L., 1932 -

   Israeli peace/Palestinian justice

   Includes bibliographical references.
   ISBN 0-932863-15-9

1. Jewish-Arab relations. 2. Palestinian Arabs - Israel. 3. Israel - Ethnic relations. 4. Liberation theology. I. Title.

DS119.7 .A74 1994   956.94   C94-920083-2

Clarity Press, Inc.
Ste. 469, 3277 Roswell Rd. N.E.
Atlanta, GA. 30305

and

Clarity International
Ste. 253, 919C Albert St.
Regina, SK. S4R 2P6
Canada

Dedication

This book is dedicated to

Jean Are,

and to all those who have touched my life with their faith

and commitment to peace, including:

Marilyn Gwyn
Na'im Ateek
Fahed Abu Akel
Rosco Possidenti
Ben Weir
Bill Cotterman
Warren Peck
Mubada Suidan
Nancy Lawrence
Bert Weaver
Jonathan Kuttab
Don Bobb
Jim Rogers
John Hadsell
Bob Armistead

Hanna Knaz
Elias Chacour
Tony Paris
Marc Ellis
Carol Weir
Jim Beaty
Daire Hanna
Swee Ang
Don Wagner
Sandy Cleland
Dennis Madden
Jim Jennings
Jean Rogers
Virginia Hadsell
Estelle Armistead

and

R.   M.
F.   D.

and

Tom, Jr. and Carol Are
Martha Are
Jim Are
Gene Are
Billy and Jody Andrade
Betsy Reedy

ACKNOWLEDGEMENTS

I am indebted to my wife Jean, who throughout this undertaking kept calling me to "credibility." I have tried to use illustrations or accounts of atrocities that have been reported in at least two sources.

I am further indebted to Pope Paul VI, who is credited with saying:

If you want peace
work for justice

Table of Contents

FOREWORD

The mutual recognition of the State of Israel and the Palestinian Liberation Organization, and the signing of the declaration of principles on what has been called "Super Monday," September 13th, marked the beginning of a new era in Israeli/Palestinian relations. This significant step has been perceived as the beginning of a long and hard process towards a just and comprehensive peace in the Middle East region. As the future unfolds, a good number of important issues will surface successively and will need to be addressed and resolved. But when peace is finally achieved and peace treaties are signed between Israel and its surrounding neighbors, there will still be a lot of work to be done in order to effect reconciliation between the two nations which have only known violence, injustice and bloodshed.

At the same time, peace and normalization will usher in a period of critical self-examination, and the need for a new quest for the truth. Many people who, in the past, had shut their eyes to the atrocities of Israel and refused to see what was going on, might open now to hearing the truth. With renewed zeal for research, new facts will inevitably emerge. Palestinian life under occupation will need to be more disclosed, for in spite of all that has been written, Palestinians feel that so much of what they have experienced is still not known. They want the truth to be revealed.

There is a great difference between the dissemination of truth before and after the peace treaties are signed. The former suggests the need to press people to act immediately in order to end the injustice. The latter intends to help people understand better the background to the conflict. It should help them realize the depth and extent of human evil. It should help them realize that very frequently truth was intentionally withheld from them by the influential media, that many times they were kept in the dark regarding the truth of the conflict and the reality of life under occupation. Yet ultimately, the truth has a way of appearing and asserting itself. And to know the truth is to be set free to act and do what is necessary. It is in this light that I look at *Israeli Peace— Palestinian Justice.* It is, I believe, a witness to the truth. Thomas Are is a pastor who has been concerned for many years about what was going on in Israel/Palestine. He has done an enormous amount of research. He has visited the area a number of times. He has met many people across the board of political lines. And God has laid on his heart the need to share that truth which he was able to discover with others. Thomas Are writes with the passion of a pastor who is concerned about one small area in this vast universe where injustice has been rampant for the last century. He wants those who do not know to know, those who have been confused by Middle East politics to be informed clearly, and those who have blamed the victims (Palestinians) for this evil to know the facts, and then to move on his challenge for justice and peace for all the people of the area.

This is a courageous book written by a courageous man. I have known Tom for a number of years. I know that he has received a lot of flak due to his firm stand on the side of the oppressed. But he has endured the pain and sustained his commitment to that truth.

As we move into the new era of peace based on justice and mercy, we look for a brighter future of freedom and de- mocracy. Knowledge of the truth should create within us greater determination to do everything that we can to bring about healing, forgiveness, and reconciliation.

I highly recommend this book to church people as well as to others everywhere who are seeking the truth so that when they are grasped by it, they will become active peacemakers and reconcilers, thus fulfilling their role as children of God.

Blessed are the peacemakers
for they shall be called sons and daughters of God.

Na'im Ateek
Canon, St. George's Cathedral, Jerusalem
and Author of *Justice and Only Justice*

PREFACE

I first met Thomas Are in the New Mexico desert at a seminar on the Israeli-Palestinian conflict. He was one of twenty or so participants. I, along with the Rev. Na'im Ateek, facilitated the week-long discussion. Several months later, Rev. Are invited Na'im Ateek and me to continue what had become a dialogue in solidarity at his church in Atlanta.

Little did I know that this invitation was significant beyond the issues represented by a dissident Jewish thinker and a Palestinian Christian clergyman. As I discovered later, the invitation itself engendered great controversy both within and outside of his congregation. Given the media's general depiction of Palestinians as terrorists, how could an American Presbyterian pastor invite a Palestinian to speak in a church? Local Jewish organizations also had reservations, as I have never been their preferred choice to "represent" the opinion of the "Jewish community" to the Christian community.

Perhaps the controversy helped spur attendance, as several hundred people showed for our dialogue each of the three nights we were scheduled. They were an attentive audience, and critical. Their questions and comments showed that Americans, when given an opportunity to hear different views of the Middle East, would respond with intelligence and verve. Yet it was clear in this interchange that the discussion was not simply about issues in that geographically distant Middle East; the more immediate issue posed, endangering our sensibilities and complacency, was centred in America: American foreign policy and how American Jews and Christians relate to their own histories, to each other, and to the world.

This "danger" was keenly felt at Thomas Are's Church in Atlanta during the lecture series and was transported to other speaking engagements in the area after his Church series was over. I recall during drives with him to other engagements, as well as in late-night discussions in his home, considering the more dangerous dimension to these issues in relation to his own vocation as a minister and as a Christian. Too often the persona of minister and Christian are locked in a tension capable of resolution only through acquiescence or a complicitous silence. This, of course, is true for the Jewish community as well, for which the most difficult way of being faithful today is to become a rabbi.

Israeli Peace \ Palestinian Justice represents the continuation of this struggle between minister and Christian which I witnessed in Atlanta. The book's subtitle, *Liberation Theology and the Peace Process,* is appropriate in the context of the book, although not exhaustive of the issue. Through the lens of the Israeli-Palestinian issue, Rev. Are is grappling with the question of what it means to be a Christian, now, in America.

As one finds in the pages of this book, the resolution of this issue is less important then the question it raises, and the question is contextual and controversial. Rev. Are details in this book the horror of Christian anti-Jewishness as well as the Israeli abuse of power. He also details how Christian America and American foreign policy can be in complicity with injustice. Rev. Are brings this message home, for the prayers and hymns offered by his parishioners in all good faith may, upon closer examination, be mired in the blood of the innocent.

Rev. Are concludes his book by expressing his fear that by the time of its publication, his words, by virtue of ongoing events in the Middle East, may be outdated. Unfortunately, just the opposite is true as the discussion of "autonomy," or limited self-rule for the Palestinians, periodically floated by the Israelis, represents the desire for peace without justice, a victory for one which can only mean the surrender of the other. The issues broached in this book remain, and the history Rev. Are exposes is brutal and in need of reconciliation. Could it be that the just resolution of the Israeli-Palestinian conflict lies in a forward path for Jew and Christian, if we only seize the moment? Thomas Are raises this possibility in a book filled with compassion and, at times, anger. His are words that carry a price, a price which Christians and Jews must pay, but which they have yet to recognize.

MARC H. ELLIS
Author of *Toward a Jewish Theology of Liberation*

INTRODUCTION

I admit, right up front, that what I have written here may be seen as one-sided. I do not dwell on the stories of the 1972 Olympic massacre at Munich, or the 1985 hijacking of a TWA Jet liner, or the taking over of the *Achille Lauro*. These stories have been dramatized and retold on prime time television for years. Nor have I researched every incident which goes beyond legitimate Palestinian resistance to become what may truly be conceded as terrorism, though I know they exist. I am writing out of *a concern for justice for the Palestinians.*

This account may be one-sided. But *it is not overstated.* Years ago, an editor rejected a story of mine, saying, "Readers will not believe it."

"But it's true." I answered.

"Doesn't matter if it's true or not," he declared. "It has to strike the reader as believable."

As an author, I remember that rule of writing and try to abide by its logic. At the same time, what I have learned about the policies of Israel seems so unbelievable. Should I "mind my own business" and not write about oppression because it seems unbelievable?

I was advised to mind my own business when I was in about the fourth grade. I had gone with Effie to the grocery store. Effie was my "maid," my confidant and fifty years my senior. I never knew her last name. She had worked as a housekeeper for my parents since I was a baby, and I loved Effie. I don't remember what circumstances put me in the same grocery store with her early one Saturday evening, but I remember the way she tied her "pay" into the corner of a handkerchief. The clerk had placed on the counter a small bag of beans, some fat back, rice, and a pound of coffee. Effie was counting her money and thinking about what else she could afford when suddenly... "The Klan's coming!" someone shouted.

I didn't know what that meant, but his announcement excited everyone. I ran to the front of the store expecting to

1

see a circus or parade or something, and there they were. Pick-up trucks, horns blowing and lights on inside and out, exhibiting 'grand dragons' dressed in white robes with hoods over their faces, looking very frightening. I ran back to Effie. She would take care of me. But Effie was gone...she disappeared, leaving behind her groceries and her money on the counter.

"Where is Effie?" I asked the clerk.

"She won't be showing her black face around here any time soon," he laughed.

I walked home thinking, it's not right for anyone to work all week and be so frightened that she runs off and leaves her pay. Effie had not done anything wrong. Her only crime was being black in South Carolina in 1940.

The next day in Sunday School, I asked my teacher why Effie had been so afraid?

"Well, it's the way things are," he said. "We'll all do better to just mind our own business."

Even then, at eight years old, I knew something was not right. Minding one's own business is another way to say "be self-centred and indifferent." But I didn't know what else to do, so I minded my own business.

Sixteen years later in seminary, I was still minding my own business. Several of us, studying late one night, decided to go out for a cup of coffee. The only place open at two A.M. was the local Donut Shop. We raced in to get out of the cold and took a booth in the corner. As we talked, an old man came in.

"Shut the door," the man behind the counter yelled. "Old John" fumbled with his coat, and stepped up to the counter. Of course, John was not his name, that's just what I had learned to call older black men when I didn't know their names. "What'll you have?" the man behind the counter demanded.

I paid little attention to what was happening, but very soon Old John picked up a styrofoam cup of coffee, a few donuts wrapped in a napkin, and went back outside. "Shut the door," the man shouted again.

After we had finished eating, we pulled on our coats and walked out to return to school. There was Old John, sitting on the curb, pulling up his collar to block the bitter cold, and sipping his coffee. I didn't say anything, didn't know what to say, but I knew something was wrong. We had silently stepped around an old man who was not allowed to sit down in a coffee shop for no other reason than that he was black in Georgia, in 1956. We went back to our warm dorm to study theology. I had never heard of Liberation Theology, but I knew in my conscience that the oppression in which I participated had to be unacceptable to God. But I still minded my own business. Gradually, injustice to others became my business. The community where I served my first pastorate was the home of Mary Holmes, a Junior College for black students. It was a Presbyterian School, but not of my denomination. I was southern Presbyterian.

One day, I saw Dawson Horne, President of Mary Holmes in the Post Office. "Before we start shooting at each other, like they are doing in some other Mississippi towns," I said, "Why don't you and I get together and talk?" We did, off and on for six months. I learned a lot about the oppression of blacks in Mississippi. For the first time, I was beginning to understand injustice, but my meeting with Dr. Horne caused a great deal of anxiety in the church I was serving. "Not that's it's wrong," they said to me. "It's just not the thing to do."

I knew of the mistreatment of blacks in my county. Yet even then, I could hardly bring myself to speak out against injustice to a complacent congregation. I chose the safe route of dealing with my discomfort by moving to another church. Years later, when I realized how much the oppressed people of my community needed some Christian to speak up on their behalf, I vowed that if I were ever in those circumstances again, that I would stand on the court house steps and shout my head off. *I would not sit passively by, mind my own business and say nothing about injustice.*

Segregation challenged my faith. Even though the other-worldliness of God had been taught to me as the focus of worship, I could also hear the words of Jesus about Good News to the poor and liberty to the oppressed. The more I prepared sermons to comfort my all white congregation, the more uncomfortable I became with preaching them. How could I proclaim that "God loves and cares for us," without acknowledging at the same time that God also loves and cares for the black citizens of our community who washed our clothes, scrubbed our toilets, made our beds and removed

3

our trash? The stereotypes of "They are happy with it this way," and "God chose them for a lower station in life," no longer rang true. Without realizing it, I was becoming a Liberation Theologian.

Now, thirty years later, it's "those circumstances," again. I have come to believe that the Palestinians of the occupied lands of Israel today are the African-Americans of Mississippi in the 60's.

Some have accused me of choosing a safe situation of injustice so that from a comfortable six thousand miles away, I can "shout my head off, and soothe my feelings of guilt without risk." Maybe so. You, the reader will have to decide and the only way you can know is to read beyond what I have written. You'll have to listen to those Arabs, Jews, and Christians who have been close enough to the scene to know. But be careful, for if you are convinced that injustice is inflicted on vast numbers of helpless people, then you too will have to stand up and "shout your head off."

Like most North Americans, I live in a comfortable world of career, sports, and sit-coms. I do not want my world to be upset. I have insulated myself with a string of myths designed to protect me from becoming discontented. Here are four myths I had long accepted.

1 My ISRAELI myth:[*] Jewish people have suffered "forever" just because they are Jews. I have become especially sensitive to their persecution since the holocaust. If ever a people deserved a peaceful homeland where they could be defended against persecution, it was the surviving Jews of Europe. Their leaders, after the war, chose the "uninhabited" lands of Palestine. It was a perfect selection. "A people without a land, in a land without a people," they said. The few Arabs who lived there were backward, uneducated nomads who couldn't appreciate the motherland anyway. Given the advanced morality and technology of Jews, the Arabs would be better off with Jews to take care of them. It was a great plan, but something went wrong.

---

[*] I reject the holocaust revisionist's claim that the Holocaust never happened. It happened and such violation of human rights should never be forgotten. But I also reject the Zionist manipulation of the memory of that horror to justify the systematic violation of the human rights of others.

Those ungrateful Arabs, according to my myth, became jealous and resented the miracle-working Jews who turned the desert into a garden. Arabs started harassing and persecuting the Jews all over again. Arabs rose up, unprovoked, and terrorized their peace-seeking Jewish neighbors. Since that time, Israel has had no choice but to go back to war again and again just to protect her right to exist.

In my myth, I might allow an atrocity or two by the Jews here and there. National Security never comes cheap and requires that dirty deeds be done from time to time. Whatever trouble the Arabs are having, they brought it on themselves.

2 My ARAB myth: Arabs come in two classes. The upper group is made up of billionaires who own oil wells, drive limousines, and are buying up America. On the other hand, the lower ranks drive camels, carry daggers, and prey on the community. Both classes are barbaric and uncultured. They never quite made it in the civilized world and they are mad about it. They express their anger through terrorism and rising gas prices.

Where did I get such a picture of Arabs? From television. From *Sesame Street* to *Rockford Files,* TV shows seldom portray Arabs as responsible citizens. Apparently Arabs do not become doctors, lawyers, and homemakers. My media diet skipped right over Arab contributions to modern medicine, science, and art to show me sword-wielding Muslims who would just as soon cut your throat as lose face.

Someone said, "It's easier for a camel to go through the eye of a needle than for anArab to appear on television as a genuine human being."[1] I seldom saw the devout follower of Allah who stops his truck, kneels down in the heat of the day to give homage to his God.

3 My PALESTINIAN myth: Palestinians are victims of their surroundings. Brothers of other Arab nations urged them to leave home in 1948, but then would not open the door for them to immigrate. For years, Palestinians have waited for some outside hero to come along and rescue them. They dream of pushing the Israelis back into the sea, and have waited to return to the land of their ancestors. None of

5

this has happened. So they retaliate with violence in hope of attracting world attention to their plight.

When I think of Palestinians...well, they are Arabs, so I don't picture a cultured nation of authors and engineers who serve their community and love their children. I picture a trigger-happy criminal who hates his neighbors and looks like Akbar, the terrible, on Saturday Night Wrestling. Besides that, the Palestinians were offered a homeland in 1948, but they chose to go to war. My myth includes a God who sees that right always wins. So once again, David slew Goliath.

I read in *O Jerusalem,* by Collins and Lapierre, how the Palestinians ambushed a convoy of doctors on its way to the Hadassah Hospital on Mount Scopus. I heard of economic boycotts and shootings and the creation of a terrorist organization, the PLO, headed by Yasser Arafat, an outright out-of-control terroristic gangster, who insulted the world by showing us Palestinian anger. Even though none of these tactics succeeded, the Palestinians still refused to recognize Israel's moral right to exist.

They are still not happy. So, out of desperation, Palestinian mothers send their children into the streets to throw rocks at the Israeli soldiers who are, after all, just doing their duty. Palestinians are just unreasonable. So, when I hear that Israel doesn't want a state full of antagonistic Palestinians sitting on its border, I don't blame them.

4 My HOLY LAND myth: Two people have a claim to the same real estate. Neither wants to share it with the other. There is no solution. Israel claims that God gave the land to the Jews. On the other hand, Palestinians point out that their ancestors have lived on the land for thousands of years. No one can unpack these conflicting claims, so why bother? Let the Jews and Arabs settle it between themselves. After all, they have been fighting each other since the beginning of time.

Those are the myths I have lived with. Like most of my neighbors, I complain about my life, but mostly I am content, so please don't take away my myths.

In the summer of 1990, I picked up the book, *Justice and Only Justice,* by Na'im Ateek. I read it, more out of a feeling that I should learn more about the situation in the Middle

East than out of a burning commitment to justice. Yet that book and its author began to awaken within me a zeal for justice and compassion that will no longer allow me to hide behind my myths. I could no longer continue with a business as usual practice of ministry.

I wish the whole world could hear the story of Na'im Ateek. On Wednesday, May 12, 1948 eleven-year old Na'im watched the Haganah march down the street, enter house after house announcing that Beisan must be evacuated within the hour. "For your own safety," the soldiers said. No choice. Palestinians could take only what few items they could carry.

By nightfall, the Ateek family and all the other villagers had been forced into a barbed wire compound and forbidden to go home. Na'im's father pleaded with the troops to let them go back and pick up a few personal belongings, but to no avail.

In one hour's time, the Ateek family, along with tens of thousands of others, had become refugees, driven out of their homes forever. Many were killed. Some were separated from their families, never to find each other again. The Ateeks would live as second class citizens under military rule from then on.

Golda Meir defended Israel's action:

> It was not as though there was a Palestinian people in Palestine... and we came and threw them out and took their country away from them. They did not exist.[2]

In writing of that time period, historian Arnold J. Toynbee declared:

> The treatment of the Palestinian Arabs in 1947 (and 1948) was as morally indefensible as the slaughter of six million Jews by the Nazis... Though not comparable in quantity to the crimes of the Nazis, it was comparable in quality.[3]

"We were lucky," Ateek said speaking from his memory. "None in my family were killed."

Today, Na'im Ateek is Canon of the Saint George's Cathedral in Jerusalem. He says of himself, "I am a Palestinian, but not a terrorist; an Israeli, but not a Jew; an Arab, but not a Muslim." He is most of all a pastor and has first-hand awareness of the tragedy of the Palestinians he serves. In his book, he writes of:

> Severe beatings —crushing hands to prevent stone throwing, clubbing shoulders, legs, abdomens, and heads —the use of tear gas, rubber bullets, and live ammunition; arrest, night raids on houses, detentions, sieges of refugee camps, curfews, deportation, harassments, and humiliations.[4]

Frankly, I had never heard these kinds of things about Israel and it was hard to believe what I was reading. I wondered if Ateek exaggerated. Then I saw a statement signed by the heads of the Christian Communities in Jerusalem. These religious leaders, nine in all, represented the major churches, including Greek Orthodox, Roman Catholic, Episcopal, Armenian and Evangelical Lutheran. In one part, it read:

> We are particularly concerned by the tragic and unnecessary loss of Palestinian lives, especially among minors. Unarmed and innocent people are being killed by the unwarranted use of force. We condemn the practice of mass administrative arrest and the continuing detention of adults and minors without trial.[5]

These leaders pleaded for the world community to hear. I read their appeal and felt guilty. The mother church in Jerusalem was still being persecuted and like many other Christian pastors, I didn't even know about it.

As I continued to read Na'im Ateek, it touched me that he was writing from a pastor's heart and not as a politician. He believes that peace in the Middle East must come through justice and compassion, not by weapons and humiliation. His compassionate words tore away at my long-revered myths. I could hardly believe I was reading the words of an *Arab*. He was not pleading for bloodshed or retaliation, but begged for peace and justice.

I am indebted to Na'im Ateek who, without knowing it, has called me to a clarity in ministry, to a preaching that seeks justice with compassion and calls upon the Christians of the world to speak out against injustice. Christianity cannot be silent in the knowledge of oppression.

I oppose oppression of any kind and especially when it involves human torture. I take the position that the torturer is always wrong, whether considered by my government to be friend or foe. *The torturer is always wrong.*

I am not trying to write a history book. I write out of pastoral concerns. I believe that God loves every human being, regardless of race, color, or creed. Thus, no one should be oppressed, beaten, tortured, or denied the essentials of a decent life.

I don't know why an abused child so often grows up to be an abusive parent. Nor do I understand how a people so oppressed can suddenly with power become so oppressive. Someone with better psychological understanding than mine will have to figure out the why's. My hope for now is that the *abuse stops.* If the nation of Israel does not have the inner character to cease its oppression, then the world community of those who seek peace through justice, will have to force Israel to alter her present course for her own sake as well as for the Palestinians. The stain of Israel's conduct will not easily wash away.

Two notes:

1 - In several places, I have shared experiences that were related to me first hand by people living in Israel. As they told their stories, they pleaded with me not to use their names or show their pictures. Later, I asked my friend who had arranged for my visits into the Occupied Territories why they were so cautious about being quoted. "I have to use names and places and dates," I said, "for my record to have credibility."

"No," he said. "You cannot use names. These people are at great risk for even talking to you."

R., my friend, a denominational-level peace associate, went on to tell me that on one of his last trips into the territories he had been accompanied by an American who happened to be a retired military officer. He was visiting the Palestinians, not as a U.S. soldier, but as a Presbyterian elder. Later, talking to some authorities, the elder referred to the atrocities he had learned about from a family he had visited. To add authenticity, he provided their names and that of their village.

The next week, my guide told me, "The Israeli soldiers showed up at that family's home. They deported the teenage nephew, and *beat the father to death.* Do not go home and use names," R. said. "You will be safe, but those to whom you refer may suffer for it."

In most cases throughout this book, I have footnoted and tried to document all factual accounts. In some cases, however, when stories were told to me directly, I have changed the names and places for obvious reasons. Someday when Israel is more humane, maybe all of this can be rewritten as history and proper credit can be given to those whom I see as heroes of their faith.

2 - I have chosen Israel's dealing with the Palestinians as my illustration, but the principle of no peace without justice could just as equally apply to injustice in North America, South Africa, Central America, South America or any other troubled spot in the world.

Chapter One

HUMAN RIGHTS ABUSE
AS OFFICIAL POLICY

That anyone could deliberately abuse another human being is appalling. That Jews, just two generations past the Holocaust, could commit atrocities against other human beings seems impossible. Yet newspapers, magazines, Amnesty International, Save the Children, the International Red Cross, even the U. S. State Department, all speak of human rights violations. Doctors and ministers who have recently visited the occupied territories give testimony to horrible brutality. Israel's "iron fist" policy in dealing with the Intifada strikes fear in the hearts of civilized people around the world.

"Don," I asked a friend of mine who had just returned from the West bank, "Have you seen it, I mean with your own eyes? I've read about it, but it's still hard to believe."

"I have seen it," he said.

This is what he told me:

> We were driving past an elementary school during recess time. The yard was full of children. Three Israeli soldiers, hardly more than youngsters themselves, were walking across the street from the school. Suddenly a rock came sailing out of the crowd. It barely made it to the street. One of the soldiers saw it. All three charged the school yard. Kids ran screaming toward the building but the soldiers caught one child, probably the smallest and slowest in the class. He looked to be about a second grader.
>
> The little guy pleaded for them to let him go. I thought they would, but they dragged him kicking and begging to the street. They forced his hand onto a rock and as he shrieked in agony, two men held him down while the third man ground a stone back and forth over his hand until his knuckle bones were crushed.
>
> The soldiers walked away, leaving their eight-year old victim with four broken fingers, satisfied that they had protected Israel's national security from a second grade threat.

11

Israeli soldiers reason that with a broken hand, a second grader won't be able to throw rocks. I heard similar stories in May, 1990, when I attended a conference of Churches for Middle East Peace in Washington. "Can this really be happening?" I asked. A doctor there testified that while serving as a volunteer in a West Bank hospital:

> They brought in a teenage boy. Soldiers had beaten him with four foot plastic whips that had torn into his flesh. Bones could be seen through the wounds in his back. By the time I saw him, that poor kid didn't know his name, where he lived, or even why he had been beaten.[1]

These kids had been attacked, not by hoodlums on the streets, but by soldiers under orders, carrying out official government policy. These reports sounded so unbelievable. Later that year, I met Marc Ellis, co-editor of the book, *Beyond Occupation*. "You open your book with a story of soldiers breaking the legs of teenage boys. It's barbaric. Is it really true?"

"I didn't write a novel," he replied. "That account is a matter of record, testimony of the soldier involved." In 1988, an Israeli captain entered the village of Hawara and ordered the local mukhtar to round up twelve Arab boys, all teenagers. Yossi Sarid describes what happened:

> The soldiers shackled the villagers, and with their hands bound behind their backs, they were led to the bus. The bus started to move and after 200-300 meters it stopped beside an orchard. The "locals" were taken off the bus and led into the orchard in groups of three, one after another. Every group was accompanied by an officer. In the darkness of the orchard, the soldiers also shackled the Hawara residents' legs and laid them on the ground. The officers urged the soldiers to 'get it over with quickly, so that we can leave and forget about it.' Then, flannel was stuffed into the Arab's mouths to prevent them from screaming and the bus driver revved up the motor so that the noise would drown out the cries. Then the soldiers obediently carried out the orders they had been given: "*to break their arms and legs* by clubbing the Arabs, to avoid clubbing them on their heads, to remove their bonds after breaking their arms and legs, and to leave them at the site." The mission was carried out.[2]

Ari Shavit served 12 day's reserve duty in the Gaza Strip's Ansar II detention camp. Many of the prisoners are teenagers arrested for stone-throwing or membership in illegal organizations. His article about the prison appeared in the May 3, 1991 weekend supplement of *Ha'aretz*:

N., an unsentimental Likud supporter, tells anyone who is willing to listen, why this place looks like a concentration camp.

...the problem is not one of similarity. No one seriously thinks that there is a real similarity. The problem is that there is not enough dissimilarity... And maybe the fault lies with the detentions done by the Shabak: almost nightly, after interrogating a number of youngsters to the breaking point, the Shabak passes a list of the youngster's friends to the paratroopers in the city or to the Border Guard professionals. And you see them going to the curfew-bound city at night, to arrest the people who endanger the security of the state. And you see them returning- with 15 and 16 year-olds, teeth chattering, eyes popping, often already beaten and manacled. Even S., who has a factory in the occupied territories, can't believe his eyes.

'We've come to this?" he says."We've reached the point where the Shabak run after children like these?'

Or perhaps the fault lies with the screams: At the end of your watch, on the way from the tents to the showers, you hear horrible screams....from over the galvanized tin fence of the interrogation section come hair-raising human screams. I mean that literally: hair-raising. And you of course have read the B'Tselem report.... And you ask yourself, what is going on here five meters away? Is it someone being tied in the 'banana' position? Or is it a simple beating?

This sketch is from the March 1991 B'Tselem report on torture in the occupied territories. It states that the "banana" tie, commonly used during interrogation, makes the body "vulnerable to the blows of the interrogators."

You don't know. But you do know that from this moment forth you will have no rest. Because 50 meters from the bed where you try to sleep, 80 meters from the dining hall where you try to eat, human beings are screaming. And they are screaming because other people – wearing the same uniform as you – are doing things to them to make them scream.

They are screaming because your state, your democratic state in an institutionalized, systematic manner – and definitely legally – your state is making them scream...

On any one day, some 14,000 people are imprisoned; nearly one percent of the population of the territories. What is going on around you is not some sort of essential, defined and exact 'surgery' on the opposition spy network but the repression of a popular uprising. What is going on is that our entire population...is carrying out the task of imprisoning their entire population...And that is something the likes of which does not go on today in any place in the world which is called 'proper'. And you are a partner, you are a collaborator.[3]

What is this, I thought, all these stories? Israel breaking bones, causing people to scream? Israel is the people of God, the children of Abraham, the "by you all the families of the earth shall be blessed" people. (Genesis 12:1-3)

From childhood, I had heard about Israel, the chosen people of God. I loved to listen in Sunday School to every heroic story. Modern Israel, I assumed was still the chosen people, still the godly and heroic descendents. Years later, after I had become the pastor of a 1,000 member congregation, I visited Israel myself. I was shown around by an Israeli guide and I came home impressed. "I am a Zionist," I announced to my congregation. "I have seen the desert turned into a garden." After seeing the television story about the Israeli rescue at Entebbe Airport in Uganda, I said, a bit facetiously, "I vote to get the Jews to run the world. They take care of things right." I had read *The Source*, *The Exodus*, and *O Jerusalem*. Little did I realize that Leon Uris had been commissioned to write *The Exodus* for the sole purpose of creating a "more sympathetic attitude toward Israel."[4] Its propaganda design worked on me. I gave little thought to the fact that *The Exodus* was fiction. The same with the popular movie, *The Long Shadow*, which I saw at least half a dozen times. I celebrated the trial of Adolph Eichmann and watched with amazement the miracle of the Six Day War.

14

The one thing I did not do was ask about the Palestinians. For most of my life, I have promoted Israel.

But now I have changed. I have reversed on Israel at least 179 degrees. Since I have been asking questions, doing interviews with people who know, and reading documented material, my integrity has forced me to speak out about the policies of the State of Israel. The past few years have forced me to see that the State of Israel has been paid for by another people and they are still paying. As a Christian pastor, I speak out for those "other people" who have so few advocates. In the rest of this chapter, I want to point out some of the human rights abuses that directly derive from official policies of the Israeli government.

KILLINGS

Every day in the occupied territories, the Israeli military confront unarmed Palestinians who feel that anything can happen to anyone at any time for any reason. The Israelis call it security. The Palestinians call it the *Intifada*.

It started on December 8, 1987 with an automobile accident in the Gaza Strip. Four Palestinians were killed when an Israeli truck crashed into Arab cars near a military check point. "It was no accident," the Gazans said, "but rather a deliberate retaliation for the stabbing death of a Jewish man in Gaza's market." Arabs began to demonstrate. Jews began to shoot. According to Amnesty International:

> Over 540 unarmed Palestinians, including children, have been shot dead by Israeli soldiers during the first year of the uprising, often in circumstances suggesting excessive force or deliberate killing."[5]

It was self-defense, Israel said. Just soldiers trying to extricate themselves from dangerous life-threatening situations. Evidence shows, however, that the vast majority of those killed were not threatening anyone. Most were engaged in passive activities such as raising a flag, running away from hostile soldiers, or simply gathering into small groups on the street or in front of their own homes. In only three cases were those killed throwing Molotov cocktails,[6] which Israel exploits as justification for widespread violence and killing. In 36 shooting cases, Israeli soldiers actually interfered with the transportation of wounded Palestinians to the hospital. Eight of those hindered from getting help, died.[7]

The victims of Israel's "self-defense" included men, women and children. At least 52 of them (or 20 percent of all killed) were children. Some were very young children. One child in Gaza was three years old. According to the *Washington Post*, in the first 30 months of the uprising, Israeli soldiers have shot and killed 159 children and beaten thousands. More than 50,000 children have been treated for injuries, including 6,500 wounded by gunfire. *"The average age of children killed was ten."*[8] What was their crime? Heaving stones, scribbling slogans on walls, or displaying Palestinian flags. The Israeli Army blames the death of so many children on Arab militants and parents "who send their children out into the street and encourage them to become martyrs."[9]

Save the Children refutes the army's alibis and declares that Israel's formal rules barring the shooting and beating of children by soldiers have been systematically flaunted in the field. Children, in fact, do participate in the demonstrations and stone-throwing. Yet, more than half of those killed were not in the vicinity of any protest activity. Save the Children says:

> Researchers for this report have documented indiscriminate beating, tear-gassing and shooting of children at home or just outside the house playing in the street, who were sitting in the classroom or going to the store for groceries.[10]

Israel changed to rubber bullets for "humanitarian reasons," hard black rubber bullets with solid metal cores. When fired at close range, these penetrate the skull and cause serious injury, or even death. Then in September, 1988, Israel replaced the tear gas, rubber bullets and clubs with a new plastic bullet not classified as "live" ammunition. Under the new policy, soldiers could shoot to control and not just to defend themselves in "life threatening" situations. This new "shoot to punish" rule produced 47 more Palestinian deaths and 288 injuries.[11]

I hear so many statistics that they run together in my mind. But one thing is clear, the *Intifada* brought an unprecedented killing of Palestinians, most of them teenage boys and girls. Kids with rocks just don't have much chance against soldiers with guns.

I remember scenes of shootings on the six o'clock news and thinking, surely world opinion will force Israel to modify its fierce policies against helpless people. Israel apparently came to the same conclusion and responded to world opinion. However, the government did not ban the policy of shooting unarmed people. Instead Israel banned the press from reporting its brutalities. But they were too late. News clips of soldiers shooting into unarmed crowds had been seen around the world.

BEATINGS

Even though secret beating of detainees in prison had been common in Israel for years, on January 19, 1988, Defence Minister Yitzhak Rabin, later to become Prime Minister, changed the prescription by announcing the policy of "punitive beating" of Palestinians.[12] Examining 3,460 of the 7,107 documented cases of beatings by soldiers in the first year of the uprising, investigators of Save the Children concluded that one-third of beaten children were under ten years old, and one fifth under the age of five. Nearly a third of the children beaten suffered broken bones.[13]

Emotionally, there is something humiliating about being beaten. I read about young Arabs being dragged behind a building and systematically beaten all but senseless. Israeli soldiers wielding clubs put pressure on arms and legs and elbows and knees until they crack. Many of those who wind up in prison are beaten after being taken into custody. Some beatings are savage. *Newsweek* quotes an Israeli soldier:

> We got orders to knock on every door, enter and take out all the males. The younger ones we lined up with their faces against the wall, and soldiers beat them with billy-clubs. This was no private initiative, these were orders from our company commander... After one soldier finished beating a detainee, another soldier called him "you Nazi," and the first man shot back: "You bleeding heart." When one soldier tried to stop another from beating an Arab for no reason, a fist fight broke out.

The same article goes on to reveal:

> Armed with 30-inch wooden clubs and urged by the prime minister to "put the fear back into the Arabs," Israeli soldiers have methodically beaten up Palestinians since early January, deliberately breaking bones and beating prisoners into unconsciousness... Casualties included not only young men...but also women.[14]

"Our task is to recreate a barrier," says Shamir, "and once again put the fear of death into the Arabs of the area."[15] He has certainly tried. What is the government's attitude toward brutality? In the first year of the uprising, only one soldier was charged with causing a child's death. He was punished with a reprimand.[16]

HUMAN TORTURE

In efforts to gain confessions (usually of names, or belonging to a terrorist group), Israel subjects prisoners to isolation, tortures, and unsupportable physical conditions.

> Upon arrest, a detainee undergoes a period of starvation, deprivation of sleep by organized methods and prolonged periods during which the prisoner is made to stand with his hands cuffed and raised, a filthy sack covering the head. Prisoners are dragged on the ground, beaten with objects, kicked, stripped and placed under ice-cold showers.[17]

Amnesty International concludes that "There is no country in the world in which the use of official and sustained torture is as well established and documented as in the case of Israel."[18] The use of torture on Arab prisoners has been the subject of extensive investigation for years. Ralph Schoenman, past Executive Director of the Bertrand Russell Foundation, said:

> Israeli interrogators routinely ill-treat and torture Arab prisoners. Prisoners are hooded or blindfolded and are hung by their wrists for long periods. Most are struck in the genitals or in other ways sexually abused. Many are sexually assaulted. Others are administered electric shock.[19]

At Sarafand, a military camp used for interrogation, electric shock torture is used almost universally. Case after case of testimony describes such inhuman treatment as:

—whipping and beating the soles of the feet
—squeezing of the testicles
—hosing prisoners down with ice water.

One prisoner, Shehadeh Shelaldeh, arrested, interrogated and held without trial for sixteen months, tells of having "a ballpoint refill pushed into his penis." And in another instance: "Joseph Odly fell unconscious when they brought his daughter into his cell, held her down, spread her legs and shoved a stick into her vagina."[20]

These and many other tortures reported in the *Sunday Times* are similar to hundreds of testimonies reported by Israeli lawyers, Amnesty International, and the International Committee of the Red Cross. According to Thomas Freidman, Jewish author of *From Beirut to Jerusalem*, Israel regularly practices force to extract confessions from Palestinians. Even those not accused of any crime are tortured in prison.[21] The Data Base Project of Palestinian Human Rights reports:

On the first night of arrest every prisoner, without exception, is systematically hooded with a thick canvas bag pulled tight around the neck. The bag is filthy and heavy enough to impede breathing, and has severe psychologically disorienting effect on the detainee. The prisoner, already handcuffed behind the back and sometimes leg-shackled, is then chained to a hook or pole set at varying heights to make either sitting or standing impossible. The detainee can be left in this state for hours or days, without water, food or toilet facilities. He/she is sometimes drenched purposely with water and left in the cold, as well as beaten and humiliated by passing soldiers. From the 'softening up' treatment, meted out

Reprinted from B'Tselem report

to men, women, and children of all ages, whether charged

with an offence or not, physical abuse can escalate to what is defined as torture by international law. [22]

In July 1991, I talked with a Christian minister in Israel who volunteers much of his personal time to work in the camps which are under Israeli military rule. I quote:

People disappear. People go to prison. Or they are held for eighteen days incommunicado. In Israel, Palestinians have no basic rights that they can demand. In the territories, there is no real judicial system. The military is the highest authority. In the West Bank, Palestinians live under more than 2000 military laws or ordinances that the people have to comply to. These laws change and they are not promulgated. People don't even know what the laws are.

If someone is thought to be a suspicious character or a threat to the state, he or she can be put in what is called administrative detention. In administrative detention, people are usually put for six months in the desert in Ansar 3. There, they don't have any visitation rights. Lawyers also have difficulty spending time with their clients.

If you go into downtown Jerusalem, if you go by the Russian compound, there is a place called Moscobiya, which is the old Russian convent. This is basically a holding area where people are brought for interrogation by Shin Bet, the secret police. There, they are tortured. B'Tselem, an Israeli human rights group, has just recently issued a report on the kinds of torture that takes place when someone is being interrogated. There are all kinds of torture. The ones I am most familiar with from the stories that have been told directly to me and that are reported by B'Tselem are that people are put in what is called the closet. The closet is an area about two feet wide, and about

five feet tall. It's low, and there is no window. He gets light through the bottom crack in the door. Often, the person has his hands tied behind his back. There is a peg that is placed about as high as the shoulder level of the back, so his back is always hunched over. Then, at times a hood, a canvas hood is placed over his head. He is kept in this closet while he is being interrogated. It can go on for days with you in that kind of position. People are also beaten, tortured with electrical shock and so on. This goes on when they are being interrogated. Also, when people are brought to the court, the military court usually has its officer to serve as judge. And often the Shin Bet serves as prosecutor of the case.

Recently, I was in a court up in Ramallah. In this court, they were having a hearing for Dr. Mandoua al-Aker, a friend of mine. Dr. al-Aker is a Palestinian national. He is a surgeon and has worked for years for nonviolent solution of this conflict. He is known by Secretary of State, James Baker. He is an active member of Palestinian and Israeli Physicians for Human Rights and is well known for his peace activities. He also was tortured when he was being interrogated. He said the thing that bothered him most was that he was deprived of sleep for 60 hours and then became very disoriented. After that, he said that it wasn't so bad even though he was still in the closet.

Well, I went to his hearing. It was on Easter Sunday, 1991. I was allowed into the Ramallah court with about four members from B'Tselem for his hearing. He is a celebrity, so his hearing took about three hours. While we were there, and while he was having his hearing, they would bring in about six shebab (Palestinian teenage boys) at a time... and you would have the lawyers and the judge conferring back and forth. They would be sentencing these shebab; they were running them through. I don't know how many were sentenced in the three hours I was there. But their hearings took all of about two to three minutes. Usually it went something like this. They would call out the name of one of the shebab, I remember one boy in particular, about 15, and the prosecutor then tells the judge that he will settle for three months. So the judge gives this boy three months. He was accused of throwing stones. The boy said, "I didn't throw any stones." The boy had been in prison now for two months before coming before this judge. The judge said, "If you admit to throwing stones, I will give you three months and I count the other two. So you are in prison another month. If you continue to refuse to admit that you threw stones, you go back to prison and you will not appear before me for another seven months." What does he do? Continue to say he didn't do it, or does he confess and he is out in a month. This is the kind of legal system that goes on. What is also shocking for me is that Dr. al-Aker has been held for 30 days and they were never able to even come up with a charge. So, they didn't present anything to the court. By all rights, and when you are thinking logically, you would be thinking that he would be released. But the judge gave him another ten days for the Shin Bet to try to get some more information. Dr. Mandoua al-Aker stood up and asked if he could speak. He said, "If you keep me for another ten days, I won't know anything more to tell you then, than I do now." Then, right in the court, in front of two lawyers, one a Jewish lawyer from B'Tselem and a Palestinian lawyer associated with *Al Haq*, before the judge and myself, the prosecutor said to him right out loud: "You can make any statement you want, *we have ways of making people talk.*" And no one batted an eye. The judge didn't rule him out of order.[23]

Of course, Israel denies that such things happen, or claims that these are isolated incidents of extraordinary circumstances. Evidence is overwhelming that the torturers are not individuals who get out of hand. They are members in good standing of Israel's police and security divisions following orders and operating in line of duty. Israel may deny the charge, but it is irrefutable that torture is a fundamental part of Israel's legal system.

COLLECTIVE PUNISHMENT
Collective punishment means
—cutting off phones and electricity
—setting curfews on entire towns
—uprooting trees
—making mass arrests.
Collective punishment means violating due process of law and making a mockery of justice. Collective punishment means assaulting many for the suspected actions of a few. In spite of the fact that in 1985, the U.N. General Assembly "condemned Israel for its collective punishment, mass arrest and ill treatment and torture of Arabs in the Occupied West Bank,"[24] Israel still practices collective punishment. At any time of the day or night, Palestinians living in the

occupied territories are subject to mass arrest and imprisonment, to be held for long hours and often days, without
trial or lawyer.

One of the most heinous forms of collective punishment
is the demolition of homes. In the Middle East, families build
onto their houses for decades. Rooms and floors are added
as needed and afforded to accommodate several generations.
To lose a home in the Middle East brings economic and psychological devastation on an entire family. Yet Israel practices
house demolitions. The Captain on the jeep becomes judge,
jury and executioner with power to select and destroy houses.
Whole families suffer for the suspected, unproven, conduct
of a single member. Usually, home demolition takes place
between midnight and dawn. Suddenly there is a knock on
the door, followed by orders to get out, with only a few minutes to empty the house of its inhabitants and contents while
soldiers set explosives. Then, as a family watches in shock,
their home is totally and forever destroyed.

By the end of the first year of the *Intifada*, 550 homes
involving almost 5,000 people were destroyed.[25] For "security
reasons," destroyed homes are not allowed to be rebuilt. The
heartache, the emotional distress, and economic devastation
is often followed by Jewish settlers who move in and start
building. The village of Qisan near Bethlehem was almost
obliterated in October 1988 with the destruction of 30 homes
at the same time. The Israeli government said that the
Palestinians had built on land requisitioned by the military.

In Idna, near Hebron, 112 families were issued threats
with home demolition. In November of that same year, 80 to
100 homes were razed, displacing more than 400 people.
Israel admits some homes were destroyed by mistake.[26]

DETENTIONS

One of the most heinous policies for any government, much
less one claiming to be a democracy, is Israel's practice of
Administration Detention—holding people for administrative rather than judicial reasons. They make no charge; it's
just for government convenience. By the end of the first year
of the uprising, more than 5,600 Palestinians were in detention. More than six times that many have been detained for
at least some period of time. "Detention" in American usage

sounds like staying after school for talking in the library or being held up for a few minutes by the traffic cop. In Israel, it's more likely to be a violent kidnapping carried out by state-approved hostage takers, followed by a long imprisonment without charges. It's all legal. Some detainees are only twelve years old.

Mass arrest, as many as 50 in one night in the same village, results in abominable prison conditions. These conditions lead to broken bones, disease, blindness and death. The largest and most dreadful camp, Ansar 3, located in the Negev desert, is called "the camp of slow death" by Palestinians.

> It's overcrowded with up to 28 prisoners in a single tent. Latrines are flooded and filthy, washing and drinking water insufficient, food inadequate and often spoiled. Prisoners are not given clean clothes or sufficient supplies of mattresses, blankets, soap, towels, razors, or toilet paper.[27]

Try to imagine what it must be like to be arrested, tried by a military judge, convicted by "secret evidence," which neither you nor your lawyer ever get to see, and sentenced to a prison like Ansar 3 with no right to appeal. Such treatment is outrageous. But at the time of this writing, it happens in Israel.

SETTLEMENTS

The Six Day War of 1967 resulted in Israel's capture of the West Bank, Gaza Strip, the Sinai Desert, Golan Heights and East Jerusalem. Since that time, the Golan Heights and Jerusalem have been annexed; the Sinai has been returned to Egypt. But in the West Bank and Gaza, almost one and a half million people have lived now for almost 25 years under Israeli military rule. A whole generation has never known anything but the humiliation of oppression and occupation.

Most of the settlers are well educated, frontier-spirited, and willing to take the law into their own hands. They take the best land. There is no social contact between the Arab villagers and Jewish settlers. Hostilities are intense. In 1980, a band of settlers was found guilty of maiming two

Palestinian mayors on the West Bank by car bombs. Settlers have confessed to such things as:

—plotting to blow up the Dome of the Rock (the Arab mosque in Jerusalem)

—spraying the campus of the University of Hebron with gunfire

—killing three Arab students and wounding 33 others,

—planting bombs in five Arab buses, threatening 250 Arab lives.[28]

In fairness to Israel's court system, some were arrested, found guilty and sentenced. Every now and then, Israel slaps the wrist of the settlers to make the world think that Israel is a democracy with "equal justice under the law." At the same time, the territories offer Israel a dilemma. If Israel annexes the West Bank and Gaza, making all its residents citizens, Israel will cease to have a Jewish majority. Thus, Israel has chosen two simultaneous paths that will (1) give them more land and (2) have fewer Palestinian citizens to deal with.

Controlling the land by establishing settlements

On assuming office, Menachem Begin revealed his vision for the borders of Israel by changing the designation of the West Bank to the Biblical names Judea and Samaria. He promised the Knesset (Parliament) in June, 1977 that the West Bank and Gaza would never fall under "foreign sovereignty, that Jerusalem would never again be divided and would remain the eternal capital of Israel and that a Palestinian state would never be established."[29]

When Begin took office again in 1981, there were about seventy-five settlements with 18,000 settlers in the West Bank. By 1984, settlements occupied over 40 percent of the total of the West Bank with 65,000 regular inhabitants. Housing Minister Sharon said in July, 1991, "We'll put a million Jews in the West Bank."

I was in Jerusalem when Sharon made this announcement. I remember well the reaction of a Roman Catholic priest:

> These settlements are what Israel calls "creating facts on the ground." But, when a peace process moves along to a stage where we are really going to settle up with what we are going

to do, if indeed Sharon is right and there are a million Israelis here, they are not going to just pack their bags that night and leave. There is going to have to be some kind of further compromise in the West Bank. Now, these settlements are deceptive because for every settlement, there is a surrounding perimeter which is also not available to the Palestinians. In addition to that, there is a road network that is always set up between these settlements and the main roads within the West Bank and these roads also have a perimeter which is not available to the Palestinians. In the West Bank, there are also seven military governors for the seven regions of the West Bank. These military governors all have their headquarters and their perimeters which are not available to Palestinians. In addition to that are police stations, army barracks, army posts, prisons and Israeli dumps that have their perimeter as well. When you take all of that together, 60 percent of the land of the West Bank is not available to the Palestinians. This is the quiet strangulation of a people."[30]

The present goal is irreversibility—establishing a permanent Jewish presence (and Israeli control) over the West Bank and Gaza. Through a variety of means, Jewish settlements, which now make up 6 percent of the total population, have taken control of 77 percent of West Bank and 40 percent of Gaza.

Driving out the Palestinians.

The government of Israel apparently believed it could postpone dealing with the occupied territories until it had reduced the Palestinian population. Their position said, in effect, "The world will simply look on, watch, and do nothing." Ariel Sharon publicly advocated policies to encourage, even force Palestinians to move from the territories. Planning the expulsion of the Palestinians was openly discussed by many on Israel's political right.

Meron Benvenisti, former deputy mayor of Jerusalem said, "Jews and Arabs are living in the same territory, but 90 percent of the cultivatable land, 75 percent of the water and all the infrastructure is geared to supporting one of those two peoples, the Jews."[31]

One of the main problems in the Middle East is and always has been water. In an arid land, adjacent wells often compete for the same supply. Israel takes iron hand control of all well-drilling permits. Thus, Palestinians have difficulty obtaining permits while settlers have water to use and to waste. Jewish settlements look like modern suburbia with swimming pools and green lawns watered by sprinklers. Yet across town, Arabs live in squalor and without enough water to keep their vegetable gardens from dying. Jews in the territories enjoy many times over the water quota of their Palestinian neighbors.

The civil administrator in the West Bank, Brig. Gen. Ephraim Sneh, observed that "The amount of water pumped for an Israeli resident is twelve times as much as the amount pumped for a Palestinian."[32]

Israel, which has a 500 million cubic meters water-use deficit,[33] diverts water from the West Bank for use within Israel proper. The Palestinians see well drilling schemes designed to steal water, in some ways far more precious than oil, as part of a plan to reduce them to dependency and poverty. They believe that when they get weak enough, Israel will grind them to dust and blow them away.

For the same reason and in the same way, Israeli taxes collected from the West Bank and Gaza have been greater than the amount spent by Israel in services and infrastructure. Beit Sahur, a town of 10,000 located a few miles from the traditional site of Shepherd's Field near Bethlehem began a tax revolt in 1989. "No taxation without representation," they cried.

To crush the revolt, the Israeli Defence Forces closed Beit Sahur to all outsiders, including the media, and began to expropriate property. James Wall, a keen observer of events, wrote in the *Christian Century*:

> If Beit Sahur were Peoria, Illinois, or Woodward Hills, California, and refused to pay its taxes, most American citizens would sympathize with the government's decision to confiscate property and force payment. But would we sanction a military blockade, the cutting off of food supplies, its severing of telephone lines, and a refusal to permit visits from international representatives?[34]

On October 6, 1989, the United Nations General Assembly condemned Israel's occupation policies with specific references to raids for the purpose of confiscating property for back taxes. The resolution passed 140 to 2. The United States and Israel cast the only two negative votes.[35]

Israel's policy of "take over and harass" includes Jerusalem, which is the emotional heart of the three faiths of Judaism, Islam, and Christianity. In spite of Israel's guarantee of "full access to holy sites within the city," Al-Haq, winner of the Jimmy Carter Foundation Human Rights award, has documented Israel's repeated use of tear gas and rubber bullets against worshippers at Jerusalem's Dome of the Rock. Because some Muslims were brave enough to risk such injury, military road blocks make Jerusalem's holy sites inaccessible to many West Bank Palestinians.[36]

The official policies of all the world's governments do not recognize the annexation of Jerusalem. Yet Palestinians are regularly refused permission to construct new buildings, and they cannot obtain permits to make necessary repairs to existing buildings. Large tracts of land have been expropriated around Jerusalem for subsidized Jewish settlements. The Associated Press declares "Israel now admits paying to put Jews on Christian Site."[37]

The government, after first denying it, finally admitted that it had put up $1.8 million (which later proved to be U.S. money) to establish a Jewish settlement in the Old City's Christian Quarter. This settlement of 150 Jews in the St. John's Hospice in the Christian Quarter of Jerusalem, not far from the Church of the Holy Sepulchre, is all a part of Israel's plan to extend Israel's control over the Holy City.

Another expression of Israel's harassment of Palestinians is reflected in the dual legal system which exists in the occupied territories. Israeli settlers are subject to civil law. At the time of this writing, Arab Palestinians are governed by *military* law. The military uses all kinds of measures to protect the privileges of the Israeli settlers and to harass the indigenous Palestinians. Among military tactics are rigid censorship, mass arrest, administrative detentions, the torture of prisoners including children, collective punishment of families and whole villages, destruction of houses and the deportation of dissidents, including those who advocate nonviolent resistance.

International legal opinion demands that the Geneva Convention rules apply to Israel's conduct in the West Bank and Gaza. The basic theme of the Geneva Convention, to which Israel is a signatory, charges occupying forces to protect persons under occupation. It prohibits:

—individual or mass forcible transfers, as well as deportations of protected persons from occupied   territories... regardless of their motive,(Article 49)

—collective punishment, reprisals against persons or their property, all measures of intimidation,(Article 33)

—any measure of brutality, (Article 32)

—unlawful confinement or deprivation of rights of fair and regular trial. (Article 147)

In the judgement of Amnesty International, Israel violates every one of these regulations.

Ironically, Israel justifies her abuse by recalling the Defense Emergency Regulations that were brought into being during the period of the mandate by the British. These were 120 sweeping orders enacted to cope with tense situations during the final days of British authority. These regulations were bitterly opposed in 1946 by the Federation of Hebrew Lawyers in Palestine as giving far-reaching power to authority without due process of law. Britain revoked these regulations before the War of Independence because they were too harsh. Yet these same regulations were adopted by Israel two years later and applied to Arabs in Israel until 1966. Since 1967, Israel has enforced them against Arabs in the Occupied Territories. Since 1967, under these regulations, the Israeli military has issued over 2,400 laws to be applied to Palestinians, with no regular system of appeal. Judges are appointed by military commanders. Evidence gained by torture is admissible. The judge makes the only record of what occurs in court. Between 1967 and 1988, over 250,000 individuals have been arrested and taken to Israeli prisons, detention centers, and police stations. According to the Red Cross, ninety percent were arrested for the purpose of eliciting information.[38]

Israel's plan to take over a territory, to pressure the expulsion of a people, and her treatment of helpless Palestinians is so blatantly immoral that it prompts Christians all over the world to join the Presbyterian Church (PCUSA) in calling upon Israel to:

1 - Cease the systematic violations of the human rights of Palestinians in the occupied territories. Specifically we call for an end to the policies and(or) practices of administrative detention, collective punishment, the torture of prisoners and suspects and the deportation of dissidents.

2 - End the policies and(or) practices of beating and using food and fuel embargos in the attempt to subjugate and break the will of the Palestinian population, thus ending resistance to Israeli control of the occupied territories.

3 - End the settlements policy and the acquisition of land within the occupied territories, since these simply provoke the Arab people and reduce the opportunity for a peaceful resolution of the conflicting claims of Israel and Palestinians.

4 - End its occupation of the West Bank and Gaza as part of a larger peace process.[39]

The United Nations and even the United States, which seldom utters a critical word against Israel, have declared Israel's occupation of the West Bank and Gaza Strip to be "illegal."

I pray for Israel and hope she reforms and survives as a nation. But I am no longer a Zionist. Because of the unacceptable policies of Israel, I have made at least a 179-degree turn in my thinking.

Chapter Two

JACOB: THE DARK SIDE OF DAVID

For over forty years, Israel has projected itself as the clean-cut, faithful-to-God David, forced to fight with a slingshot the uncivilized giant, "Goliath," with the big bad sword. A closer look at little innocent David and... well, when David grows up, there is another side to him, not quite so innocent.

David was a strange kind of a man. In spite of a few big sins like adultery and murder, he was known as one after God's own heart. He was a political genius and he knew when to look the other way. We can't understand David unless we know about Joab. David could sing his songs, say his prayers, and walk softly through Israel because he had Joab to make the wheels turn.

Joab was David's personal enforcer. He was strong, ruthless and completely loyal to David. His mode of operation was force. Joab seldom did anything by negotiation if it could be done a bloody way. And David needed him. Joab, the commanding general of the army of David, hated Abner, the commanding general of the army of Saul. He stood in the way of what David wanted most. Abner, the most influential man in all the northern tribes, was the only man who could keep David from possessing all the land. Abner was invited by David to come as his guest to visit and talk about the future of Israel. Abner came under a flag of truce and agreed to negotiate (sort of a land for peace agreement). Abner conceded that David could be king of Israel and Judah. But then Joab came home. "Come Abner," he said. "I want a word with you." Abner, assuming that the truce of David also applied to David's general, came unarmed to meet Joab. As the two of them stepped through the gate into the darkness, Joab pulled a dagger and killed Abner.

The one man who could keep David from ruling all Israel had just been wiped out by David's highest ranking general. King David called for a funeral and commanded a mourning. He cried and delivered a sermon. David publicly mourned for Abner. He kept on crying until all Israel was convinced that David did not really desire the underhanded death of Abner. Everybody considered David innocent. But, could it be that Joab knew all along that David wanted Abner dead or he would have been rival to David for the land forever. The kingdom would have no security. David cried, "O Joab, he is too hard for me, his ways are too rough for me." But David never disciplined Joab. The general was never fired. David sang his songs and said his prayers and walked softly through Israel like the righteous king, precisely he had Joab to be his hatchet man.

Another time, David sent Joab out to contain Rabbah, where there had been a rebellion. Joab had all the strength, the men, and the power as he marched into the city. He raped. He murdered. He destroyed. He showed no mercy. "He ravaged Rabbah," the Scriptures say. He wiped them out. And again David cried. "O Joab. He is too hard for me." But David never removed Joab from power.

DOES ISRAEL PRETEND TO OPPOSE TERRORISM WHILE JOAB CARRIES IT OUT?

As far back as 1948, Israel considered terrorism a legitimate method of persuasion. The Histraduth, a Zionist Trade Union led by David Ben-Gurion, "terrorized Jewish shops and factories who dared employ Palestinians. Jewish women were attacked in the market place for buying from Palestinian merchants. Palestinian fields and vineyards were vandalized. Orchards were guarded to keep out all but Jewish workers."[1]

One of the most notorious acts of terrorism was the bombing of the King David Hotel in Jerusalem, by Menachem Begin's Irgun, which killed ninety-one people. During the time of the War of Independence, thousands of Palestinians became refugees because of military terrorist tactics. I always thought the Palestinians fled their country in response to a call by Arab leaders to get out and in spite of Jewish efforts to persuade them to stay. But evidence shows that Arab flight was prompted mostly by Israeli political and military leaders who believed it necessary to "transfer" Arabs out of their country in order to have a Jewish State.

In 1961, the Irish journalist Erskine Childers examined the American and British radio monitoring records and found

"There was not a single order or appeal, or suggestion about evacuation from any Arab radio station inside or outside Palestine in 1948."[2] On the other hand, Zionist radio stations had been broadcasting in Arabic urging Palestinians to leave home.[3] An Israeli officer revealed just how deliberate the broadcasts were:

> ... as uncontrolled panic spread through all Arab quarters, the Israelis brought up jeeps with loudspeakers which broadcast recorded "horror sounds." These included shrieks, wails and anguished moans of Arab women, the wail of sirens and the clang of fire alarm bells, interrupted by a sepulchral voice calling out in Arabic: "Save your souls, all ye faithful: The Jews are using poison gas and atomic weapons. Run for your lives in the name of Allah."[4]

Zionist history describes the methods of terrorism used to attack the Palestinians... The objective was to "inflict physical harm" or "liquidate them." Terrorist bombs were to be placed in "clubs, cafes, and other meeting places, communication centers, flour mills, water plants and other vital economic installations."[5] Examples of Israel's state terrorisms and condoning of terrorism by its surrogates are numerous, but three snapshots of Israel's history deserve consideration: Deir Yassin, Lebanon, and the *Intifada*.

Deir Yassin

On April 9, 1948, in the struggle to rid the land of Arabs, the Stern Gang headed by Yitzhak Shamir, and the Irgun headed by Menacham Begin, conducted the massacre of an Arab village called Deir Yassin. Jews claim 100 people were killed. Arabs say it was 250.

These acts of violence were designed to frighten Arabs into fleeing for their lives. It worked. The commander of the Haganah, Zvi Ankori described what happened at Deir Yassin:

> I saw cut-off genitalia and women's crushed stomachs...It was direct murder. Soldiers shot everyone they saw, including women and children. Parents begged commanders to stop the slaughter, to please stop shooting.[6]

No one denies that most of those slashed to death were women and children. Jewish terrorists shot people in their homes and threw their bodies into the streets as a message to neighboring Arab villagers. Survivors of the raid tell stories of Israeli soldiers starting to kill early in the morning and continuing all day. They killed everyone they saw, including old people and children. Anyone they found, they slaughtered. One pregnant woman had her stomach cut open with a butcher's knife.[7]

The attack on Dier Yassin dramatically widened the gulf of hatred and fear that separated Palestinians and Jews. Zionists say it was not terror, it was war, even justified by their Scriptures. "We had no alternative...we were just defending our land.[8] Begin himself wrote:

> Out of our evil, however, came good. This Arab propaganda spread a legend of terror among Arabs and Arab troops, who were seized with panic at the mention of Irgun soldiers... In the results it helped us. Panic overwhelmed the Arabs of Eretz Israel. Kolonia village...was evacuated overnight... Beth-Isla was also evacuated."[9]

Deir Yassin was not alone. Village after village felt the sting of Israeli massacres. Unwanted villages were destroyed. Out of more than 550 Arab villages in the territory occupied by Israel, only 121 remained. The rest were bulldozed. In the first wave of immigrants, approximately 200,000 Jews moved into abandoned Arab houses. Jewish children played with the toys that Arab children had left behind when expelled from their homes.

By the end of the fleeing, only 165,000 of the over 800,000 Arabs remained in Israel. Many were forced to march in blood soaked-clothes through the streets of Jerusalem past jeering on-lookers, never to be seen again.[10]

Lebanon

By 1954, Israel had plans in hand for the absorption of parts of Lebanon. According to Moshe Dayan, Israel just needed to buy an officer, "just a major." This puppet leader would invite "Joab" into Lebanon. The major would head a government and Israel would capture Lebanon and expel the Palestinians who had taken refuge there.

On Sunday, June 6, 1982 at 5:30 a.m., Israel unleashed Joab. Bombing began and continued for ten days: cluster bombs, concussion bombs, high flame incendiary bombs, and white phosphorous bombs. The invasion's purpose was to scatter the Palestinian population through massacre and terror, to create a panic, and to convince the Palestinians of Lebanon that they were not safe in that country either. Israel spoke of "Peace in the Galilee," but it was Joab all the way.

The Canadian ambassador said Israel's bombing of Lebanon "would make Berlin of 1944 look like a tea party... it is truly a scene from Dante's Inferno."[11] John Chancellor of NBC said, "I keep thinking of the bombing of Madrid during the Spanish Civil War... we are now dealing with an imperial Israel."[12]

The terrorism that stirred even the conscience of Jews in Israel was the slaughter of the unarmed citizens of the refugee camps of Sabra and Shatila. By Sharon's own admission, Israel planned the massacre months before allowing the Christian Militia into the camps. Bashir Gemayel, with whom Israel collaborated, had informed Israeli officials that he would raze the camps and flatten them into tennis courts. Israel knew exactly what would happen. Gemayel's forces had been trained by the Israeli army.[13] Again, Joab did his job.

Major Etienne Saqr, who took credit for the massacre with the Israelis, explained, "No one has the right to criticize us; we carried out our duty, our sacred responsibility."[14] Elie Hobeika, Intelligence Chief for Gemayel's militia described his massacre:

> Shoot them against the pink and blue walls; slaughter them in the half-light of the evening. The only way you will find out how many Palestinians we killed is if they ever build a subway under Beirut.[15]

During the first few months of the 1982 invasion of Lebanon, 20,000 Palestinians and Lebanese, mostly women and children, died, 25,000 were wounded and 40,000 were made homeless.

The invasion of Lebanon also produced many Israelis who were vocal in their opposition to the aggressive war in

Lebanon. In July 1982, approximately 100,000 Israelis marched through the streets of Tel Aviv demanding the withdrawal of troops from Lebanon. When it became known that the slaughter by Christian Phalangists of some 700-800 men, women and children in the Sabra and Shatila camps had the full knowledge, support and encouragement of Israel's army— the crowd of protestors grew to 400,000.

The Intifada

If there was ever a question of Israel's commitment to Joab's iron fist methods, it has been removed by Israel's terroristic response to the Intifada. Bassam Shaka'a, deposed Mayor of Nablus, describes the brutality of Israeli soldiers in his town:

> Convoys of buses cruise the streets of Nablus followed by vans of the Mossad, Israel's secret police. Army units go from house to house pulling youths from their beds at 3 a.m. As the buses fill, the soldiers beat the youths viciously around the head, shins, groin and back. Shrieks fill the air.[16]
>
> Among the victims were the grandmother of the Da'as family and the hundred year old father of noted Nablus attorney, Mohammed Irshaid. Soldiers had entered the house at 2 a.m. smashing furniture and firing a canister of a dreaded green gas while preventing the family from leaving.
>
> Two children, ages nine and eleven, were taken by the soldiers in their night clothes, frog-marched in the streets and beaten as they were forced by the jeering soldiers to clear debris.
>
> Simultaneously, the Israeli army targeted the hospitals. Army trucks rammed ambulances and blocked them from reaching the homes of those overcome by gas. Soldiers entered the Ittihad Hospital in Nablus numerous times, arresting the wounded and those waiting to give blood to family members. Even the operating theater was invaded while surgeons were operating on patients.
>
> Doctors were beaten and equipment smashed. Family members were prevented from entering the hospital and cars of doctors and nurses were destroyed by soldiers."[17]
>
> In the Balata camp outside Nablus and in the Casbah -- the old quarter --a thousand people were arrested in a period of forty eight hours. The discovery of people in ditches in the fields--shot in the back or with their heads caved in --has been reported from villages throughout the West Bank and Gaza.[18]

While David cries innocent, Joab terrorizes the land. I always thought that the new-born Israel faced the onslaught of five Arab armies as David faced Goliath with a numerically inferior, poorly armed people in danger of being overrun by a military giant. I always thought Israel's victory of 1948 was a miracle. But it was just another massacre.

DID ISRAEL PRETEND TO FIGHT
A DEFENSIVE WAR IN 1948

On Jaffa Street, Jerusalem, can be seen a small statue of a homemade rifle used by Jews in their fight for independence. The rifle is little more than a tin pipe and scrap metal, but it represents an image of little David's slingshot, and by implication poor infant Israel having to defend her very existence against the powerful armies of five Arab nations committed to Israel's destruction.

The Israeli army was *not* outnumbered. Arab States committed a small part of their arms to the war, but they were largely at cross purposes with one another. On the other hand, Britain had promoted the destruction of the Palestinian economy. The mandatory government granted a privileged status for Jewish capital, awarding it 90 percent of the concessions in Palestine and enabling Zionists to gain control of the economic infrastructure, such as road prospects, Dead Sea minerals, and electricity. When in 1936-1937 the Arabs called for a general strike, Britain arrested most of the Arab Higher Committee and forced the Grand Mufti to flee the country, depriving the Arabs of many of its best leaders. The British underhandedly prepared Israel for war by stripping the Arabs of their weapons while at the same time assisting in training the army of the Jewish Defense Forces.

Charles Wingate, an expert in terrorism and assassination techniques, trained the Haganah including Moshe Dayan, in the use of large, destructive barrel-bombs and how to force Palestinian men to confess to crimes by shoving fistfuls of sand down their throats.[19] By 1939, Zionist forces included ten well armed groups of Colony Police, each commanded by a British officer, and all with an official Jewish leader second in command. By early 1944, the Zionists had some 43,000 Jews in military service. Many belonged to the Haganah, made up of 60,000 to 70,000 trained members which became the backbone of the Israeli Army. Some 20,000 to 25,000 had served in various Western military forces during World War II.[20]

The Irgun and Stern Gang had several thousand troops each. Also, some 30,000 new immigrants selected carefully with the war effort in mind entered Israel between May 15th and August 9th, 1948.[21] Jews had been integrated into British intelligence and actually became police enforcers. Such a "quasi-police" force provided cover for British training of 12,000 men organized into the Haganah and 3,000 in the Urgun. Add to those numbers the foreign volunteers with military and technical skills, Jews and non-Jews from 52 different countries; all in all, within a few days of the outbreak of the war in 1948, Israel had 60,000 better trained and better equipped troops in the field than the 25,000 troops of the Arabs.[22]

Even before World War II, Jews had begun to acquire illegal weapons. Munitions were stored in Europe. Shortly after the Mandate expired, 30 shiploads of men, food and munitions left European and other ports for Israel. On the nights of May 14-15, these ships began entering Israeli ports.[23]

Another key to Israel's advantage was the UN agreement for a 28-day truce starting in June. During that time, Israel was able to accumulate arms and reorganize her army. When war resumed, Israel took the lead. By this time, David had a bazooka. By the end of the truce, the Arabs had 45,000 troops at most, compared to an estimated 100,000 soldiers available for Israel.[24]

I always thought the Arabs totally rejected partition and responded to the call of the Mufti of Jerusalem to all out war which forced Jews to military action. The truth is, many Palestinians were seeking peace. It was Ben-Gurion's opposition to a Palestinian State that left the Arabs with no choice. Israel was convinced that it could win more on the battlefield than at the peace table. By the cease-fire in January 1949, Israel had much more land than the UN Partition Plan had granted. But three key areas, West Bank, Gaza Strip, and Golan Heights remained under Arab control. For that, Joab would have to wait until 1967.

IS DAVID CRYING PEACE
WHILE JOAB IS FIGHTING FOR LAND?

What Ben-Gurion wanted has been in little doubt from the very beginning. His territorial ambitions were spelled out: "The boundaries of Zionist aspiration include southern Lebanon, southern Syria, today's Jordan, all of Cis-Jordan (West Bank) and the Sinai...After we become strong as a State, we shall abolish partition and expand to the whole of Palestine."[25]

In 1948, when General Yigal Allon asked him, "What is to be done with the population of Lydda and Ramle?" — some 50,000 inhabitants — Ben-Gurion, according to his own biographer, waved his hand and said, "Drive them out." Today, no remnants of Lydda and Ramle remain. This area is totally occupied by Jews. Upon the occasion of Ben-Gurion's first visit to Nazareth, he looked around in astonishment and said, "Why are there so many Arabs, why didn't you drive them out?"

The Palestinians were driven out. Between November 29, 1947, when the United Nations partitioned Palestine, and May 15, 1948, when the State was formally proclaimed, the Zionist militia had seized 75 percent of Palestine, forcing 780,000 Palestinians out of the country.[26]

Moshe Dayan told Zionist youth at a meeting in the Golan Heights in July, 1968:

> Our fathers had reached the frontiers recognized in the partition plan; the Six Day War generation has managed to reach Suez, Jordan, and the Golan Heights. This is not the end. After the present cease fire lines, there will be new ones. They will extend beyond Jordan....to Lebanon and...to central Syria as well.[27]

To drive off Palestinians has been the Zionist plan all along. Back in 1940 Joseph Weitz, head of Jewish Agency's Colonization Department which was responsible for settlements, said:

> Between ourselves, it must be clear that there is no room for both people together in this country. We shall not achieve our goal if the Arabs are in this small country. There is no other way than to transfer the Arabs from here to neighboring

countries — all of them. Not one village, not one tribe should be left.[28]

The Koenig Report stated Israel's policy more bluntly: "We must use terror, assassination, intimidation, land confiscation and the cutting of all social services to rid the Galilee of its Arab population."[29] Israel says, "We want peace," but Joab plans elimination: "It is time to rip away the veil of hypocrisy. In the present, as in the past, there is no Zionism, no Jewish State, without the removal of all Arabs, without confiscation."[30]

In 1984, the political platform of the Labor Party advertised the "Four No's:

—No Palestinian State,

—No negotiations with the PLO

—No return to the 1967 borders, and

—No removal of any settlements.

The advertisement went on to advocate an increase in the number of settlements in the West Bank and Gaza.[31] According to the *Washington Post*, February 7, 1988 under the headline, "Expelling Palestinians," two Israeli journalists disclosed an Israeli cabinet discussion in 1967 on resettling Arabs. Begin recommended the demolition of the refugee camps and the transfer of Palestinians to the Sinai. Others disagreed, thinking that Syria or Iraq may be better places, or even the Sinai desert. At any rate, the *Post* article states that a secret unit was set up charged with "encouraging" the deportation of Palestinians for foreign shores."[32]

Financially secured by the Jewish Agency, Zionist leaders became more open in expressing their goals. March 24, 1988, Ariel Sharon stated that if the Palestinian uprising continued, Israel would have to make war on its Arab neighbors. The war would provide "the circumstances" for the removal of the entire Palestinian population from inside Israel and from West Bank and Gaza.[33]

Yet to many Americans, the series of Arab-Israeli wars of the past 40 years have been used to justify Israel's behavior including its territorial expansions.

SECURITY BECOMES THE COVER

In all of modern Israel's history, security has been the catchword to screen widespread massacre of civilian populations, for expansions into surrounding territories, for confiscating of Arab lands, the establishment of settlements, for deportations and for sustained torture of political prisoners.

Yet Moshe Sharett, former Prime Minister of Israel (1954-1955), revealed that "Israeli political and military leadership never believed in any insuperable Arab danger to Israel. They sought to maneuver and force the Arab states into military confrontations which the Zionist leadership were certain of winning so Israel could carry out the destabilization of Arab regimes and the planned occupation of additional territory."[34]

It is not my purpose in this book to punish Israel for its oppression, but to look at what is happening. Since 1948, Israel has been living a lie. Jews are now waking up to the fact that while their leaders have pleaded innocence like David, their Zionist military has deceived them like Joab. Many young Israeli and American Jews have assumed that Israel has always been the innocent victim, that terrorism, military strikes and unfair treatment were always things that happened *to* Israel, rather than were committed *by* Israel.

Israel's only hope for survival is through justice. Joab's methods never work, at least, not for long. They always come home. As they did for David, they will for Israel. Remember Absalom, David's son who rebelled against him. David with all his power and experience said to Joab: Don't harm Absalom. But Joab slithered out on that limb and stabbed Absolom to death with his own bare hands.

David cried, O Absalom, my son, would God I had died for you. The slaughter permitted to Joab always comes home.

Chapter Three

ARGUMENTS/COUNTER-ARGUMENTS

"I disagree with you, Tom," a friend said when hearing about Israeli atrocities for the first time . "I would like to hear the other side." He went on to say, "I hear a streak of anti-Semitism in you."

Bob wrote to me out of concern for fairness and with a heart that finds it difficult to believe anyone could deliberately hurt another human being. He wrote:

> I think you are terribly wrong in your sympathy for and allegiance to the Palestinians. Your view of the situation in the Middle East is ill-informed. Also, I need to raise the issue of anti-Semitism. Criticism of Israel or its policies is not *per se* anti-Semitic. But, people blame all Jews, or at least all Israeli supporters, for every misdeed that they see Israel has committed. When you imply that Israel's support in Washington is "paid for by PACs," that is anti-Semitism. It declares that if the Jews want something, they bribe or buy someone off. I would point out that U.S.aid to Israel, military and economic, is no simple gift. Israel is the U.S.'s only reliable strategic ally in that region.
>
> I think it is grossly unfair for you to apply a higher standard for Israel than you do for other nations. I think you have been manipulated by the anti-Israel media more than you realize. I notice their distortions all the time. Every time a Palestinian on the West Bank stubs his toe, it's front page news: "Palestinian stubs toe, Israelis believed responsible."
>
> How would you like to live in a country where every neighbor is committed to your destruction? Israel can't survive if it is bound to uphold a moral standard that it's enemies can disregard.
>
> Surely you can understand at least a little why Israel would be more than a little nervous having a Palestinian state next door.
>
> And.... after all, Israel is the only democracy in that whole region. I agree that Israel should not violate human rights. But these are extraordinary times and crisis times always call for extraordinary measures.
>
> Your cavalier comparison of the Israelis to the Nazis is outrageous and offensive. It demonstrates how you see the

situation in strictly black and white terms, pure good versus pure evil, with Israel as the black evil. If there was ever an issue that was shaded in murky grays, it is this one. I hope none of this affects your duties as a pastor. For your sake, the sake of your congregation and God's sake, I hope you will not dissipate your energies on this issue. It's a political matter, not a spiritual matter. You have got to keep Church and State separated. I hope you have the wisdom to keep religion out of politics.

Sincerely,
Bob

I know Bob's love for people and I respect his concern for peace in the Middle East, so I feel a need to respond to his charges.

ARE CRITICS OF ISRAELI POLICY ANTI-SEMITIC?

It's wrong to regard well-founded and documented criticism of the state policies of Israel as Jew-bashing. Many Jews are far more emotionally concerned about what's happening in Israel than I am. They fear that Israel is on a suicide course and will not stop unless forced to do so by the U.S. or some internal awakening. I don't believe there has ever been a people so powerless for so long who, suddenly coming into power, have abused it so flagrantly. So much so, that some very highly-respected Jews are saying, "Stop the abuse."

Bob can write me off as "a partisan Palestinian advocate and a zealous anti-Zionist." But what is he going to do with notable Jews who condemn Israel such as Jacobo Timerman, famed Jewish publisher, who came to international attention as a victim of torture by the Argentine military:

> In these past months I have left behind many illusions, some fantasies, several obsessions. But none of my convictions. Among all these things, there is one that shatters me beyond consolation. I have discovered in Jews a capacity for cruelty that I never believed possible.[1]

Other Jewish leaders share Timerman's condemnation of Israel. Alexander Schinder, President of the Union of American Hebrew Congregations, sent a telegram on January 23, 1988 to Chaim Herzog:

I am deeply troubled and pained in sending you this message, but I cannot be silent. The indiscriminate beating of
Arabs, enunciated and implemented as Israel's new policy to
quell the riots in Judea, Samaria, and Gaza, is an offence to
the Jewish spirit. It violates every principle of human decency. And it betrays the Zionist dream."[2]

Albert Vorspan, Senior Vice President of the Union of
American Hebrew Congregations, wrote on January 12, 1988:

Beyond any issue in recent years, American Jews are trau-
matized by events in Israel. This is the downside of the eu-
phoric mood after the Six-Day War, when we felt ten feet tall.
Now, suffering under the shame and stress of pictures of Israeli brutality televised nightly, we want to crawl into a hole.
This is the price we pay for having made Israel an icon - a
surrogate faith, surrogate synagogue, surrogate God.[3]

In March 1988, a half page ad appeared in the *New York
Times* signed by Israeli and American teachers, writers, and
intellectuals under the heading of "Israel Must End the
Occupation:"

There can be no solution to the problem in which Israel
finds herself so long as rule by force is exercised by Israel
over the Arab populations of the occupied territories. To
present the problem as merely a matter of the necessary use
of force to restore order is an evasion of the core of the issue... We cannot and must not tolerate situations in which
our young soldiers find themselves forced to open fire on
demonstrations of civilians, many of them mere youths. The
refusal of the government of Israel to face up to the root causes
is both immoral and futile. We call upon the Government to
take immediate steps toward political negotiations...[4]

Even Rabbi Irvine Greenberg, scholar and framer of Holocaust Theology says:

Many people are devastated when they see Jewish hands
dirtied with the inescapable blood and guilt of operating in
the world. The classic Jewish self-image – the innocent, sinned
against sufferer – is being shattered. Who imagined the day
that to re-establish order, Jewish soldiers would deliberately

beat Arabs on the hands? Or smash arms and legs of civilians, not just terrorists.... The truth is painful and must be faced.[5]

Many people, including Jews, have compared Shamir's Israel with Hitler's Germany of the 1930s, Israel's occupation regulations to the policies to Nazism, and the Palestinians of today to the Jews of yesterday. Michael Lerner, editor of the Jewish Journal, *Tikkun*, writes:

> Israel's attempt to regain control of the refugee camps by denying food to hundreds of thousands of men, women, and children, by raiding homes and dragging out their occupants in the middle of the night to stand for hours in the cold, by savagely beating a civilian population and breaking its bones -these activities are deplorable to any civilized human being. That they are done by a Jewish state is both tragic and inexcusable. We did not survive the gas chambers and crematoriums so that we could become oppressors of Gaza.[6]

Of the Israeli government, Lerner demands:

> Stop the beatings, stop the breaking of bones, stop the late night raids on people's homes, stop using food as a weapon of war, stop pretending that you can respond to an entire people's agony with guns and blows and power. Publicly acknowledge that the Palestinians have the same right to national self- determination that we Jews have, and negotiate a solution with representatives of the Palestinians.[7]

The Central Conference of American Rabbis' Executive Committee issued a statement, "The policy of deliberate beating is beyond the bounds of Jewish values."[8] According to the *Los Angeles Times* poll, American Jews, by a majority of four to one, want some formula that would quell the violence. Two thirds of those polled call for some form of accommodation with the Palestinians. "Almost half of those who expressed opinions, 41 percent, were willing to admit that 'there is an attitude of racism involved in the attitude of Israelis toward Arabs."[9] Eleven retired generals – among them Aharon Yariv, former head of military intelligence, and Motti Hod, past commander of the Air Force – insist that the future of Israel requires withdrawal from the territories.[10]

An advertisement placed on the back cover of *The Nation*, July 9, 1990 by the Jewish Committee on the Middle East, expressed the concern of some American Jews including Professors at over 135 universities who strongly oppose Israeli policies.

Israeli government policies are forcing Jews to choose between the power of Israel and the religion of Judaism. Bob calls me one sided, but at least I expressed concern for the Jews and even for the security of Israel. On the other hand, Bob did not express even one ounce of concern for the Palestinians. I am encouraged by his agreeing that something should be done about the human rights violations. I am also convinced that he is unaware of just how heinous those violations are or he could not be so philosophical about them. I can't describe the beating of Palestinian children until they are senseless, and the deliberate breaking of bones as simply "unwarranted force." This kind of conduct is inhuman and cannot be tolerated by the civilized community. Saying so does not make me or any of Israel's Jewish critics de facto anti-Semitic.

Anti-Semitism is a charge designed to discredit the critic rather than address the criticism. Stand up and be counted as one who questions Israel's treatment of her minority Palestinian population and immediately you are subject to being called anti-Semitic. Even President Bush has been branded a "liar and an anti-Semite who is conducting a political fight on the backs of millions of Jews." The President's crime: his delay in considering Israel's $10 billion loan guarantee request.[11]

The charge of anti-Semitism is a vicious, angry smear that cannot be disproved. The label anti-Semitic has nothing to do with the facts or conduct. It hooks into the emotions and somehow gets interpreted as one calloused to the horrors of the holocaust. Even when it is obviously not true, the charge of anti-Semitism is impossible to disprove. Ron Carroll, a newspaper columnist, writes of the frustration of trying to prove a negative:

> I was called an anti-Semite. It's a cheap libel because it's so impossible to refute. Try it yourself. I've just called you an anti-Semite. What do you do now? I hope you didn't say that some of your best friends are Jewish. That was revealed long

ago as just another euphemism for anti-Semitism. So what else? Remember, I actually praised the contributions of Jews to 20th century culture; that was seen by more than one correspondent as proof of my sneaky tactics. Doesn't help to be a Jew, by the way; anti-Israel Jews are frequently told that they are filled with "self-loathing." Doesn't help to be anything; the word is an all-purpose cudgel now. You can't even point out the unfairness of it. That's called "blaming the victim."[12]

To criticize Israel in America today almost guarantees the label of anti-Semitism, but that does not make it so.

DOES ISRAEL HAVE A HIGHER MORAL STANDARD?

"Why does the world put a higher standard of morality on Israel than on anyone else?" a student asked. "It's just not fair." We were attending a lecture at Georgia State University by Rabbi Walter Zanger of Jerusalem. He had dismissed Israel's treatment of the Palestinians by saying, "The standard of living for the Palestinians has never been so high." He painted Israel as the most benevolent nation on earth. Every time his description was challenged, he responded by pointing to the record of some other nation. He dealt with every question by, "Well, what about South Africa," or "What about Iraq, or Russia", or "You forget how you Americans treated the Indians." It was in the context of declaring Israel's innocence that a young student raised the question of higher moral expectations for Israel. His reasoning was along the lines of:

> A normal country—let alone one like Israel that is constantly threatened—will not survive if it ties its hands with absolute moral structures and does not adjust to the pressure of power and the threats posed by its enemies... Those who insist that Israel must live by absolute morality are simply perverting morality, turning it into a battering ram for destruction. If you insist that Israel's right to exist depends on its being perfect then you are making common cause with the anti-Semites. If your self-image as a Jew demands that Israel never be morally compromised, in whatever way, then you are making common cause with the anti-Semites.[13]

Some admit that Israel is called to a high morality, but they claim that this standard is something Israel chooses to do voluntarily and should not be expected of Israel from outsiders. Irvine Greenberg says:

> If Israel proves to be ten percent better ethically than the rest of the world, it will be a "light unto the nations." If it proves to be twenty-five percent better, it will bring the Messiah. If it is fifty percent better, it will be dead. No one and no group can survive in this world if they act fifty percent better than the rest of humanity. Therefore, to insist on perfection - that Israel must never fail the higher standard - is to deny its right to exist.[14]

It's amazing that some writers are concerned that Israel might be in danger of living by too high a moral standard. We should not expect Israel to live by a higher standard than other nations, but neither should we think cultured people should tolerate standards so much lower than other nations. The Jews destroyed all but 121 Arab villages to declare Israel's democratic, higher standard of morality, statehood. Given Israel's treatment of the Palestinians since the day of statehood – the massacres of Sabra and Shatila, deliberate breaking of bones, invasions of operating rooms by soldiers during surgery, soldiers returning from duty in theWest Bank and Gaza reporting how following orders requires them to beat little children and the elderly – to claim Israel operates by an average, let alone a higher standard of morality is ludicrous.

The prophets, however, did hold Israel to a special standard."You only have I known of all the families of the earth; therefore I will punish you for all your iniquities." (Amos 3:2) Ignoring the scriptural mandate, "When you come into your land, do not oppress the ger (the stranger) who dwells in your midst" (Exodus 23:9) and "One law shall be for you and the ger" (Leviticus 19:33), Israel has chosen the power of the state over the morality of Judaism. Political Israel had a scriptural injunction to care for the widow, the orphan, and the stranger. For a people who put so much stock in some unclear mandates about land possession, it seems strange but very profitable, for the modern State of Israel to ignore so many other texts about moral treatment and responsibility for the needy and the stranger in the land.

IS ISRAEL DEMOCRATIC?

Israel may be governed by an elected parliament (the Kenesset) but other fundamental pillars of its policy profoundly contradict the democratic spirit. When Stewart Lowengrub, representing the Anti-Defamation League of B'nai B'rith in Atlanta said publicly that all Israel wants is to be a totally democratic *purely Jewish* nation, I asked, "Don't you feel a little conflict in that goal?" "Not one bit," he answered.

His answer failed to deal with the fundamental democratic postulate of equality of all people, and Israeli State policy toward the non-Jewish people of Israel. His answer failed to deal with one question which is important for Israeli democracy: *What about the Palestinians?*

In the occupied territories, there is not so much as a pretence of democracy. Palestinians don't even have right of appeal against the judgments of military courts. They don't have right to the land on which they live and farm. According to Israel, even the Geneva Convention has no influence in the occupied territories. A true democracy has a government that at least purports to represent all of the people, not one group of them against another. It's true that the Knesset has a few (six) Arab members. Out of their total Arab population, a few get elected to the governing body. But why only six? Because in Israel's idea of a democracy, Arabs are not allowed to organize into political parties. When Arabs "become political" I was told during my last visit to the Jerusalem, their house permits and other legal documents are re- inspected. Vote non-Jewish and you are harassed.

When I think of a democracy, I think of a nation that:
    a) Does not officially discriminate by religion
There is much evidence that religious minorities in Israel are treated as second class citizens. Such prejudice seems unavoidable in view of certain interpretations of Hebrew Scriptures. God is presented as the God of Abraham, Isaac, and Jacob. He is a tribal God who grants privileged status to Israel only. He elected the Jews and promised them the land. He did not elect the Palestinians, or Christians, or Muslims. According to their view, Jehovah disenfranchised everyone but the Jews.

Dreams to create a real democracy in the Holy Land where there is a national identity that embraces all the people living in the state, regardless of religion, were squelched. Israel's goal is to be a "purely Jewish nation." Religious pluralism within a secular democratic state for Jews, Christians and Muslims such as democratic America takes for granted, is not even discussed by the Zionists. The problem with a purely Jewish State is what happens to those who are not Jews. For too long Israel has followed the policies of "harass" and "drive them out."

b) Does not squelch the press

Most Americans would say that a free press is essential to the fabric of a democratic state, yet Israel has banned journalists from the territories since the first few months of the *Intifada*. More than once, cameramen have been assaulted by soldiers. The heads of thirteen Christian Churches issued a public statement taking a stand against injustice and oppression, but "When the statement was circulated to all East Jerusalem Arabic Newspapers, the Israeli censor prevented its publication."[15] In addition to print censorship, Israeli soldiers committing excesses did not like the image portrayed by the media on television, so journalists were expelled from the territories.[16] The press is not free in Israel.

c) Does not promote or indulge in terrorism

Since 1948, every cabinet of Israel has in one way or another carried out policies that would terrify me. Dr. Ghada Talhami who was born in Jerusalem and is now professor of political science at Lake Forest College, Lake Forest, Illinois, says:

> Although Israeli sources claimed in their latter years that the creation of Israel was a legal action sanctioned by the U.N., in reality, Jews were able to maximize their control over certain areas of Palestine *by resorting to terror tactics* before the Partition Plan. They continued to do so by defying UN arranged truces during the ensuing war. The pre-state Jewish terror campaign, which included attacks on civilians, is too well known to merit more than passing mention. Underground para-military organizations like the Haganah, the Irgun and the Stern Gang engaged in a flagrant campaign that included the sinking of the *SS Patria* in 1940, a ship

loaded with Jewish refugees, in order to force the lifting of the British ban in illegal Jewish immigration to Palestine. In a little-known article by the current Prime Minister, Yitzhak Shamir, which appeared in *Hehazi* (Summer 1943), voice of the Stern terrorist gang, Shamir gave a startling justification of terror: "Neither Jewish ethics nor Jewish traditions can disqualify terrorism as a means of combat... We have before us the command of the Torah, whose morality surpasses that of any other body of laws in the world: "Ye shall blot them out to the last man."[17]

Any time whole corps of soldiers engage in battering away at defenseless civilians "to break their bones," as Rabin remarked on television, it is an act of terrorism, even if it's called National Defense. A state cannot be called democratic when it permits or promotes terrorism and violence, whether conducted by individuals acting alone, by small guerrilla groups, or by its official military force against a portion of its citizenry.

d) Does not discriminate by law

Bedrock to a democracy is one law and the same law for all of the people. However, in the occupied territories, Israeli settlers live under the civil law of Israel while the Palestinians live under military law. Within Israel itself, Palestinians are deported or detained by Israel without due process and without appeal to any supreme court. Shimon Peres, Israel's Foreign Minister in 1987, said concerning deportations: "The Israeli government or the Israeli army is operating under two different laws - the Israeli law, that does not permit deportation, and the Jordanian law which recognizes deportations as a very important punishment."[18] Hundreds of thousands of Palestinians have been expelled and denied any right to return.

Likewise, since 1985, the Israeli government has practiced administrative detention. This allows Israel to arrest and hold any Palestinian for up to six months without bringing any charges. Then, the worst part, the part that would never be allowed in any democracy, Palestinians are tried by "secret evidence" in groups, and sentenced to prison. Neither the accused nor his lawyer are ever allowed to see the evidence against him. To reveal evidence might expose the secret means by which the Shin Bet had gathered it, they say.[19]

Military courts provide a means for Israel to carry out selective terrorism under the veneer of a clean legal process. "Punishment" of entire families is common.

On suspicion of throwing stones at an Israeli vehicle, Tariq Shumali, aged 16, was arrested on May 13, 1980. He was beaten so severely that he had to be hospitalized for internal kidney hemorrhage. No other member of the family was charged or suspected of any wrong doing. Nevertheless, his father was jailed, his sister was dismissed from her job as a teacher in a public school, the Shumali house in Beit Sahour was sealed off, and the family was forcefully deported to a deserted refugee camp in Jericho and ordered to make their new home in one of the dilapidated houses in the desolate conditions of the camp, which had been abandoned since the 1967 war. The intent of the authorities was to make the Shumali family an example.[20]

The collective punishment of a whole town or village for the suspected act of a few is not uncommon. Entire villages have been placed under curfew, had phone services cut, food supplies destroyed, houses wrecked, furniture smashed and parents beaten in the presence of their children.[21] Collective punishment without due process applied only to Palestinians, never to Jews, no matter how grievous the crime, equals two sets of laws for two sets of people. It sounds more like slavery in pre-Civil War *Roots* than a government "for all the people."

e) Does not violate the Geneva Convention

The U.N. Security Council voted unanimously against Israel's deportations. Resolutions 607 and 608 (January 5 and 14, 1988) deplored Israel's policies and practices in the occupied territories and affirmed the applicability of the Geneva Convention. Like numerous U.N. Resolutions denouncing Israel, this too has been ignored, with U.S. support. In fact, Israel's iron-fisted control of the West Bank and Gaza is in total opposition to the spirit of the Geneva Civilian Convention. The Convention considers individuals under the occupation of a foreign state to be 'protected persons.' Such people are protected from: physical pressure for the purpose of obtaining information; collective punishment; individual or mass forcible transfer; destruction of property not necessitated by military operations; and changing the status of public officials.

When I think of a democracy, I think of a nation that is built on justice. When I think of a democracy, I do not think of Israel.

SHOULD RELIGION BE KEPT OUT OF POLITICS?

"But, Tom. I don't think the church should get involved in political matters." Bob said. "I hope you keep church and state separate."

It may well be the case that for *my* sake, I need to tone down, but not for *God's* sake. God who loved the "least of these," calls me to keep quiet no longer in the face of U.S.-supported torture and violation of human rights. Stop the killings and beatings and then we can go back to having church picnics.

Chapter Four

RELIGION AND POLITICS MUST MIX

Even my Session, the elders of the church I had served for twenty years, voted down an invitation to Na'im Ateek, author of *Justice and Only Justice*, to preach at our church.

"It will split the church," they argued. "It would be best if he would not preach here."

"He is known as a radical," someone added.

Finally someone else broadened the issue to the mixing of religion and politics. "I come to church to hear about the Bible," she said. "As a theologically-trained minister, you have a right to talk to us about religion. But when it comes to politics, what Mr. What's-his-name has to say is just his opinion and I don't want to hear that from the pulpit."

I left that Session meeting saddened and disappointed. Na'im Ateek is Canon of the Saint George Episcopal Cathedral in Jerusalem. Last summer, President Carter worshipped in his church. One of our own adult Sunday School classes had studied Ateek's book and I had used it in officer training with elders elected to the very Session that rejected him. When my elders voted down Ateek, only six out of thirty-six had even read his book.

Warren spoke out. "If we are to be the church, we cannot sidestep the call of Christ to be a witness on behalf of justice," he said. "The church must be the church." For a moment, I thought he was going to sway the session and protect the invitation to Ateek. Then someone announced that two pro-Zionist groups in Atlanta had listed Ateek as a radical.

The vote was thirty to four. Ateek and I lost.

How could they deny the platform of the Lord's pulpit to such a man, I asked myself? But I already knew the answer. We had been duped by the doctrine of separation of church and state which asserts that whatever the governments do is none of our business. The local Zionist groups didn't like him. Therefore he was too "political" for us, no matter what his message. In fact, we were so anti-political that I had been warned that if I even prayed "political prayers," that I was going to cause "half of our congregation to leave." The possible results were spelled out to me. Members of my staff would lose their jobs. Our food pantry, street ministry, housing for humanity and world missions would suffer for lack of funds. "You have to decide, Tom, if your political agenda is worth destroying this church," I was told. "This congregation will not tolerate politics from the pulpit."

Uncle Sam had been good to the people in my upper middle class congregation and nobody wanted to condemn the goose that lays golden eggs. It's unpatriotic. But what the session was actually saying to me was *we want no politics from the pulpit but popular politics.* As long as preachers affirmed the war with Iraq, praised President Bush and sang "God Bless America," it was okay to be political. But criticism of U.S. support of Israel implies that America is either dumb, wrong or bad.

Nobody on my Session would have knowingly been a part of human torture. Yet because we did not know, we remained silent partners to some of the most atrocious violations of human rights in the world. We had chosen to believe the myth of innocent Israel, probably because we still felt guilty from the holocaust.I can't blame my Session. We live in a political atmosphere influenced by a strong Israeli lobby. Even presidents have acted against their conscience for fear of losing political support. Members of Congress are heavily dependent upon the contribution of the American Israeli Public Affairs Committee (AIPAC) and cannot "afford" to speak or vote against Israel. So how could I expect my Session to be uninfluenced by pro-Israeli propaganda?

I did not take the concerns of my colleagues lightly. They and I loved our church, and for the reasons just stated, their predictions of its demise may well have been accurate. These fears were expressed by those who had served the church faithfully for years, but they were those who had also grown up on a steady diet of the false dictum that *religion and politics don't mix.*

"There's a wall separating church and state...Reverend," Lillian said to me, "and you had better learn to respect it."

Lillian posed one of the most difficult questions facing today's church. What does faithfulness look like? To whom is the mission of the church directed? Are we called to serve the church, or do we risk upsetting the church to proclaim justice to the world?

Jesus said that we should "Render to Caesar the things that are Caesar's, and to God the things that are God's." (Mark 12:17) But just what things are Caesar's? The God/Caesar tension has been around for a long time and we are still working on it. Since the beginning, the church has debated the power of God with the power of the state...and been forgiven by God and persecuted by the state.

THE CHURCH ARGUES WITH ITSELF

Nobody knows when to birthdate the church. Some trace it back to the Garden of Eden, or even to the mind of God. However, most would agree that the church as we know it, an institution with all the problems of any other institution, was in existence at least by the time of Pentecost. Disciples gathered in an upper room, suddenly greeted by the sound of a rushing mighty wind and tongues of fire, moved out into the streets and began to preach. And already we have the problem of church and state. As long as Rome saw Christianity as one more little Jewish sect like the Pharisees or Essenes, Rome felt little threat. But suddenly, Peter was in the streets... and refusing to say, "Caesar is Lord." Peter, in the midst of Roman power, refused to put the state above the church. Rome took notice.

The Roman empire, spread over many lands, represented many cultures and languages. One way to control all those people was by emperor worship. No one actually believed that Caesar was a god, but everyone was expected to say it. Then along came those stubborn Christians saying, "Jesus is Lord." Not Caesar, but "Jesus is Lord." Rome was furious. It was not so much a matter of faith; it was treason and insurrection, a matter of politics. Rome decided the church had to be extinguished, and that could best be done by persecution.

But persecution actually made for a stronger church. To be a Christian in those days was a capital offence. People united with the church because they had encountered God and their experience with God meant more to them than life itself. Christians chose discipleship in spite of political persecution.

Persecution also helped the church grow. Those Pentecost disciples could no longer stay on Main Street, Jerusalem. They went underground, moved out into the world and, being the kind of Christians they were, created new churches everywhere they went. Like throwing hot coals onto dry leaves, they started little brush fires of dedicated communities, faithful to God above Rome. Within a few centuries, secular writers were saying: these Christians are everywhere, in our shops, in our schools, in our homes. They are turning the world upside down.

Then something happened. In 323, Constantine was converted and for whatever reason, Constantine made Christianity the official religion of Rome. Then everything changed. No longer did people join the church because of commitment to God. They became Christians by law. Suddenly the responsibility of the church was to please Ceasar, not God. The church was supported by taxes and clergy were on the state payroll. This marriage of church to Constantine lasted for a thousand years during which time it was usually far more state than church. The discipleship of putting Christ above Caesar was swallowed up in hierarchy, vestments, ritual and identity with political power. The church submitted to the government.

For more than a thousand years, whether subject to execution for being too Christian, or for not being Christian enough, Christians enjoyed little of what we call religious freedom. During those years, there were brief times when power shifted back and forth between church and state. When the government was weak, the church prevailed. When the church was weak, the state dominated. But when the church was strong...well. Pope Gregory VII excommunicated Henry IV of Germany, left him standing barefoot in the snow outside the Castle of Canossa for three days before granting him entrance or forgiveness.

The church claimed that faithfulness to God meant loyalty above any government. Christian leaders began calling upon the followers of Jesus to disobey the law of the land by refusing to serve in the army. Better to be executed for disobedience than to compromise the Christian's call to "love your enemies" and "turn the other cheek," they said. How can a Christian fight for a government that persecutes the church, they asked? How can a Christian ever submit to the state? Men, women and children faced death rather than offer the least token of worship to the emperor. It was during this time that monks separated themselves from the world, pulling away into monasteries, trying to preserve some semblance of the simple faith of those first disciples who followed Jesus.

Martin Luther: Separation

Martin Luther was one of those monks. Luther nailed his ninety-five theses to the door of the Wittenberg Church, saying that in these ninety-five ways, the church had deviated from the teachings of Scripture. In so doing, Luther kicked off the Reformation, which among other things struggled with the question of the separation of church and state. While renouncing the authority of the Pope, Luther called for Christians to recognize the exalted position of the state. He saw a sharp dualism separating the realms of religion and politics, and felt that the church should not mix into politics. He felt the devil was behind the efforts to mix the sword of the state, which is rule by the fist, with the sword of the church, which is rule by the Word. They must remain severed and separated.

> We shall learn to separate the spiritual and temporal from each other as far as heaven and earth, for the Pope has greatly obscured this matter and has mixed the two powers.[1]

To Luther the state was of little ultimate importance. The emperor could sentence a thief to be hanged, but he could not damn souls. The state merely influences that which is temporal and material while that which is influenced by the church is eternal.

> When the temporal power does wrong, it does not create a danger so great as does the spiritual power when it does wrong; for temporal power can do no harm, because it has nothing to do with preaching and faith and the first three commandments...Therefore temporal power is a very small thing in the eyes of God and is far too slightly regarded by Him that for its sake, whether it does right or wrong, we should resist, become disobedient and at odds with it.[2]

On the other hand, while Luther thought that the church had its own business he also felt that "The church should never submit in cowed silence to the abuse of power by the state."[3]

John Calvin: Cooperation

Then came John Calvin, known for his emphasis on pre-destination. Not all Christians today believe that some are elected and others rejected. But most of us respect Calvin's emphasis on the sovereignty of God which, among other things, declared Christ to be Lord of all spheres of life. Calvin put God above nations, seeing God as Lord of the church, and Lord of the State. Sovereignty laid claim to a theology of politics. Civic duty, said Calvin, integrates religion and politics. (Looking at Calvin's Geneva, we see a cooperation). Whereas today it seems the goal of politics is to protect the advantages of the rich, Calvin taught that the state control-led life to protect the poor. He personally started industries for the unemployed, helped regulate business to protect the weak, established relief services for refugees, free education and city-run medical services.

John Calvin claimed a strong role in government, and was granted a high degree of religious influence. He saw an ideal marriage between church and state:

> Civil Government is designed, as long as we live in this world, to cherish and support the external worship of God, to preserve the pure doctrine of religion, to defend the constitu-tion of the Church, to regulate our lives in a manner requisite for the society of men, to form our manners to civil justice...and to establish general peace and tranquility."[4]

We live in two worlds under two kinds of governments, one spiritual and the other political. Calvin committed him-self to improving the human condition and preached against wealth. He died a poor man. The conscience, this medium between God and man, should never be politically bound. Calvin advocated civil disobedience if the state asked for the support of practice outside the will of God, for God alone is sovereign. In addition to its unique spiritual responsibili-ties, the church had to serve the public. It lobbied on behalf of the poor to establish justice. Calvin always believed that

God's glory was expressed in the world of farms and factories operating in cooperation with the state.

TWENTIETH CENTURY MENTORS
Dietrich Bonhoeffer: A Lutheran

Early in his life, Bonhoeffer accepted the Lutheran view of separation of church and state. However, the evil of Hitler's Germany caused him to modify his position. It was not an easy decision. No one knows how much Bonhoeffer knew about the atrocities and killings by the Nazis or how soon he learned about the mass exterminations, but the news of brutality and torture aroused him. He heard of unbelievable things. What was happening in Bonhoeffer's Germany was worse than most of the world could imagine. National Socialism had become a religion, inspiring many young people to racial pride. To Bonhoeffer, it was national paganism dressed in Christian clothing.

Having visited America, Bonhoeffer recognized with appreciation the involvement of the church in the political arena, especially in the Social Gospel. When he returned to Germany, he found his Lutheran traditions mostly detached from the sufferings of people. He preached:

> He who has found God has also found his brother. The face of his brother is seen as the face of God. And he who does not find his brother, does not find God either. For God himself has become our brother in Christ, in order that we might see him behind every brother.[5]

Bonhoeffer raised his voice against the persecution of the Jews. He attacked the nationalistic tendencies of his own church, saying:

> Let the fellowship of the church examine itself today and see whether it has given any token of the love of Christ to the victims of the world's contumely and contempt, any token of that love of Christ which seeks to preserve, support and protect life. Otherwise, however liturgically correct our services are, and however devout our prayer, however brave our testimony, they will profit us nothing, nay, rather, they must needs testify against us that we have as a Church ceased to follow our Lord. God will not be separated from our brother: he wants no honor for himself so long as our brother is dishonored.[6]

Bonhoeffer organized an illegal underground seminary of ministers to serve the Confessing Church, which took steps to set itself against Hitler. Bonhoeffer helped write the Barmen Declaration which says in effect that Christians will serve the state only so far as such service does not contradict prior loyalty to Jesus Christ:

> Just as Christ Jesus is the pledge of the forgiveness of all our sins, just so – and with the same eagerness – is he also God's mighty claim on our whole life; in him we encounter a joyous liberation from the godless claims of this world to free and thankful service to his creatures. We repudiate the false teaching that there are areas of our life in which we belong not to Jesus Christ but another lord, areas in which we do not need justification and sanctification through him.[7]

Hitler never asked the church for its approval. He only asked the church to remain silent. "Leave politics to me! Mind your own business! You just prepare people for heaven."[8] Hitler was counting on traditional Lutheranism to keep church and state separated. Bonhoeffer could not peacefully sleep through the horrors of Hitler's racism. As in a nightmare, Bonhoeffer felt himself pulled into active resistance. He conspired with others in an attempt to assassinate Hitler. This was no easy decision for him. It not only pushed against his separation heritage, it confronted the Biblical command "You shall not kill." (Exodus 20:13) With blood on his hands, how could he ever preach again? The agony of mixing religion with politics carried for Bonhoeffer a judgement of great price. And he paid it. On April 9, 1945, Bonhoeffer was hanged by the defeated and vindictive Nazis.

Martin Luther King, Jr.: A Calvinist
Martin Luther King, Jr. had a dream that the world could be free of racism.

> God has a great plan for this world. His purpose is to achieve a world where all [people] will live together as brothers [and sisters] and where every [person] recognizes the dignity and worth of all human personality.[9]

61

Because of his faith in God, King trusted in the ultimate victory of good over evil. "The moral arc of the universe is long," he often said. "But it bends toward justice." His commitment to nonviolence was founded on the premise that all men and women are created in the image of God and are therefore fundamentally good, that even an evil person can be converted by love.

King, a Calvinist, seemed to have no hesitation to involve himself in the political arena. In December 1955, when Rosa Parks refused to move to the back of the bus in Montgomrey, Alabama, King called for a boycott. In two days, 40,000 black citizens snubbed the city bus lines. King said:

> It is not enough for us to talk about love. Love is one of the pinnacle parts of the Christian faith. There is another side called justice...justice is love correcting that which would work against love.[10]

Again, he said:

> We cannot in all good conscience obey your unjust laws, because non-cooperation with evil is as much a moral obligation as is cooperation with good.[11]

For months, Montgomery was crippled by actions targeted against the economy by black leaders who would not "stay in their place."

"How can a man who stirs up so much trouble claim to be religious?" white Christians asked. "He is maladjusted."

Yet even when, in the name of order, or decency, or religion, someone placed a bomb in King's house, he preached to calm the black citizens of Montgomery and continued his call to turn the other cheek. But he would not quit his preaching.

> There are some things in our society and in our world to which I'm proud to be maladjusted, which I call upon all people of good will to be maladjusted, until the good society is realized. I never intend to become adjusted to segregation and discrimination. I never intend to adjust myself to economic conditions that will take necessities from the many to give luxuries to the few. I never intend to adjust myself to the madness of militarism and the self-defeating effects of physical violence.[12]

In 1963, at his call, some ninety thousand people marched on Washington. The crowd stretched from the steps of the Lincoln Memorial to the Washington Monument to hear his immortal *I have a Dream*. King took his religion into the streets and into the offices of political leaders because he knew "Freedom is never voluntarily given by the oppressor; it must be demanded by the oppressed."[13]

> Let us march on poverty, until no American parent has to skip a meal so that their children may eat. Let us march on poverty until no starved man or woman walks the streets of our cities and towns in search of a job that does not exist.[14]

Over the years, those who are blessed by the status quo have had little motive to address the political order with religion or any other demand for change. Those who suffered have sought justification in the Bible and common sense to work for a change toward justice and opportunity. Christians on both sides of the dilemma have searched the Bible to support their own position. And both found arguable grounds. But the wall of separation has been breached too many times to be very strong.

THE BIBLE ARGUES WITH ITSELF

One reason the church argues with itself is because the Bible is not clear. Ask the Bible for its direction on the relationship of Church and State and we get mixed messages.On the one hand, David refused to harm King Saul because he was "the Lord's anointed."(I Samuel 24:10) This sounds like: if you are a king, it is because God put you on the throne and no one should touch you. On the other hand, Elisha calls for the assassination of King Joram, who likewise in the providence of God had been anointed king. (I Kings 9)

Before giving the ten commandments, God announced to Moses that God alone was to be king. The ten commandments were the laws of God, not of some king. Therefore, after defeating the Midianites, when Israel wanted to make Gideon a king, he refused by saying, "The Lord will rule over you." (Judges 8:23) Then later, when the people again asked for a king, God changed his mind and had Samuel anoint Saul. So the question remains. Are kings appointed by God? Of course, we believe Jesus was, but his was a kingdom of a different sort. "Not of this world," he said. Yet Rome was not so sure. Over his cross was written, "King of the Jews."

Paul in Romans says, "Let every person be subject to the governing authorities. For there is no authority except from God, and those that exist have been instituted by God. Therefore he who resists the authority resists what God has appointed and those who resist will incur judgment." (Rom. 13:1-2) The government that Paul knew best had the power to put him to death, and probably did. Because of this text, some would say that no matter what the state does, God has set up the authority of those in power, and the church, without question, should obey. Yet, right after Romans 13:1-2, we read, "Love does no wrong to a neighbor; therefore love is the fulfilling of the law." (Romans 13:10) The sum of the law is love. Where acts of government contradict the spirit of love, which is preeminent?

The writer of the Book of Revelation condemns the government as "the mother of harlots," (Revelation 17:5) and celebrates her downfall as a good thing. Early Christians endured persecution, proclaiming "We must obey God, rather than men." (Acts 5:29)

No wonder Christians are confused.

All the way through, the Bible argues with itself about the allegiance of God's people to the kingdoms of this world. All the way, that is, until the submission of human kingdoms celebrated in the *Hallelujah Chorus* when "The Kingdom of the world has become the Kingdom of our Lord and of His Christ, and he shall reign forever and ever." (Rev. 11:15)

The tension of the Bible is reflected in the Church. Sometimes kings have appointed bishops: at other times, bishops have anointed kings. States have executed church leaders, and church leaders have executed state leaders. Sometimes church and state have loved each other as brothers. At other times, they have fought like enemies. But the one thing church and state cannot do is build a wall to separate them, no matter what some people think the Constitution says.

THE CONSTITUTION AND
SEPARATION OF CHURCH AND STATE

In 1802, Thomas Jefferson spoke of a wall when writing to the Baptist Association of Danbury, Connecticut. Referring to the First Amendment to the Constitution, Jefferson wrote that the American people "declare that their legislation should make no law respecting an establishment of religion, or prohibiting the free exercise thereof," thus building a wall of separation between church and state.[15]

For years, we have credited the blessing of all our religious freedom to that wall. Yet the phrase "Separation of church and state" cannot be found in the Constitution; neither can the word church, or for that matter, the word God. What the Constitution does say is: Congress shall make no law respecting an establishment of religion or prohibiting the free exercise thereof. The idea of a dividing wall took root much later in 1947, in the Supreme Court case of *Everson v. Board of Education:*

> Neither a state nor the Federal Government can set up a church. Neither can pass laws which aid one religion... over another. Neither can force nor influence a person to go to or to remain away from church against his will or force him to profess a belief or disbelief in any religion. No person can be punished for entertaining or professing religious beliefs or disbeliefs, for church attendance or non-attendance. No tax in any amount, large or small, can be levied to support any religious activities or institutions, whatever they may be called, or whatever form they may adopt to teach or practice religion. Neither a state nor the Federal Government can, openly or secretly, participate in the affairs of any religious organization or groups and vice versa. In the words of Jefferson, the clause against the establishment of religion by law was intended to erect a wall of separation between Church and State.[16]

Could the court really have meant it? Build a wall between church and state? If so, could we swear in court witnesses with "so help me God," or have military chaplains, or clergy to visit death row? And what about financial aid for church-related colleges, or a Bible on which the President takes the oath of office? Could the fire department even come and put out a blaze in my church? The truth is, the court really didn't mean it. In fact the same court which prohibited prayers in school opened its session praying, "God save the United States of America."

The Constitution's intent appears to focus on keeping the state from interfering with religion. It does not say that the affairs of state could not be criticized from a religious perspective. The "vice versa" above refers to institutional control rather than the right of moral persuasion.

Separation didn't work. The Supreme Court modified its "Wall" statement, saying, "We find no constitutional requirement which makes it necessary for government to be hostile to religion."17

What this means is that Uncle Sam is not going to tell you where to go to church, or put you in jail if you don't go. It means that your tax money will not be used to build someone else's church. All of this limits the state's power over the church. But it says nothing about what churches can or cannot do to express their faith. In fact, its very statutes declare that the state cannot tell the church what to do. It simply says that there shall be no national religion; no religion shall be institutionalized by the state, with its dictates forced upon the people. It says nothing about a *wall of separation*.

Of course, some right-wing fundamentalists have tried to convince us otherwise. Pat Robertson tells how "our forefathers gathered on the beach to claim this land for God." (He fails to mention that they also stole it from the Indians.) He then reminds us of the words of the Mayflower Compact in which the Pilgrims had "undertaken for the glory of God, and the advancement of the Christian faith...to plant the first colony in the northern part of Virginia."18

He was partly right. In colonial days, at least, the state wanted to get into the religion business. Some colonial states demanded certain religious beliefs, such as the inspiration of scripture, the trinity, and a literal hell. Some states required tax support for one denomination; others taxed to support another. Jamestown established the Episcopal Church as the state church, which received state support. In 1646, the Massachusettes Bay Colony passed laws against heresy, such as "denying the immortality of the soul, or opposing infant baptism." Church membership was required for public office. Roman Catholicism was the state religion of Maryland.

The problem with a state religion is that it always leads to some degree of state persecution. In 1660, Mary Dyer was hanged as an enemy of the church. In 1707, Frances Makemie was put in prison for preaching in New York without a license. It is no surprise that our forefathers, who came to this country to escape religious persecution, would draw up a Constitution guaranteeing religious freedom without penalty. Thus, the Constitution prohibits any law "respecting an establishment of religion."

THE MISUSE OF RELIGION: SEPARATION AND MIXING IN THE SERVICE OF VESTED INTEREST

Twenty-five years ago in Mississippi when the issue was Civil Rights for blacks, the church I served had well demonstrated an inability to deal with the evils of racism. We sang hymns and studied the Bible surrounded by a people whose human dignity had been denied. The KKK and supporters of white racism harassed and oppressed the black citizens of my community, even those who were Christians. Our race separated whites from blacks far more than our faith united us. As I witnessed such abuse, I grew more and more uncomfortable with the bland acceptance of the status quo. Like my concern today for the Palestinians, any condemnation of the oppressor was met with hostility. "The church must stick to spiritual matters," I was told. They even quoted the Bible, telling me about the curse of Ham because "a slave of slaves shall he be to his brothers." (Genesis 9:25) I pointed out that it was Noah, not God who cursed Canaan. And, cursed or not, Canaan, the fourth son of Ham, inhabited the country of Judaea, not Africa.

I grew up in the Southern Presbyterian Church, which was often accused of being more Southern than church. That did not bother us. In fact, we seemed to like it. We stood up for our way of life. *I never heard a sermon on racism during all my growing up years.* It would have angered the church.

The old Southern Church, called the Confederate Church, was born on December 6, 1861 in Augusta, Georgia. The biggest issue facing the nation at that time was slavery. What should the church's role be? James H. Thornwell, one of the forefathers of my denomination, sidestepped the whole problem when he addressed the first General Assembly by declaring slavery beyond the authority of the church to discuss.

67

In the first place, we would have it distinctly understood that, in our ecclesiastical capacity, we are neither the friends nor the foes of slavery; that is to say, we have no commission either to propagate or abolish it. The policy of its existence or non-existence is a question which exclusively belongs to the state. We have no right, as a church, to enjoin it as a duty, or to condemn it as a sin...The social, civil, political problems connected with this subject transcend our sphere, as God has not entrusted to his Church the organization of society, the construction of Government, nor the allotment of individuals to their various stations.[19]

Could the fact that Jefferson both owned and sold enslaved Africans have influenced his disconnection between "all men are born equal," and his treatment of some of those equal-born who had been enslaved. Could Jefferson's theology have been economically motivated?

Immediately following the Revolutionary War, most churches condemned slavery as "contrary to the laws of God, man, and nature, and hurtful to society." The Methodists in 1784 voted to expel all slaveholders. Many Baptists expelled those who bought and sold slaves. Then, cotton became king and essential to the economic prosperity of the South. Suddenly, the church had a change of heart.

The committee... are of opinion that, under the present existing circumstances in relation to slavery, little can be done to abolish a practice so contrary to the principles of moral justice. They are sorry to say that the evil appears to be past remedy.... Your committee find that in the South and West the civil authorities render emancipation impractical, and ... they are constrained to admit that to bring about such a change in the civil code as would favour the cause of liberty is not in the power of the General Conference.[20]

Christians rejected the position that enslaved Africans were subhuman because of their theology, but allowed subhuman treatment of the enslaved because of their economic interest. For this reason, the church closed its eyes to racism.

More than a hundred years after the Civil War, when the General Assembly ordered white Presbyteries to accept Negro churches, many whites still objected. Tuscaloosa Presbytery sent an overture to the General Assembly, declaring:

God alone is Lord of the conscience, and for many members in the P.C.U.S. to obey your edict will be a violation of conscience.[21]

During this same time, I preached sermons challenging the notion that enforced segregation is the unquestioned will of God and found myself being invited to leave. The people of my church felt that they had a God-given responsibility to keep the church out of politics.

Mixing on the Right

By the 1980s, the cry for separation of church and state gave way to a deliberate effort to mix religion with politics, but the underlying motive of protecting the interest of the privileged remained the same. The Moral Majority claimed that Ronald Reagan would never have been elected President of the United States without their vote. Jerry Falwell claimed to have drawn five to eight million voters from the Democratic to the Republican party. Millions of new voters were registered in churches, sometimes right in the sanctuary.

The Christian Voice distributed more than 20 million copies of *The Candidates Biblical Scoreboard.* This voter's advocacy publication gave at least six proof texts for supporting the Contras in Latin America, capital punishment and Star Wars. It is significant that virtually every African-American senator and member of Congress rated zero on "liberal issues."

Most fundamentalists expect the imminent return of Christ and with it, the end of the world. Such a doctrine would be harmless if we were to simply wait. But many fundamentalists, claiming biblical authority,[22] predict the return of Jews to Israel, the rise of Russia, and a call to arms to defend Israel in the final battle. In his religious telecast, Robertson points to a map of the Middle East to illustrate his view of Biblical prophesy.

Jerry Falwell has received awards from Zionist groups for his support of Israel. He also believes the final war will be with Satan, when the (now defunct) Soviet Union, which Ronald Reagan called "the evil empire," invades Israel.

Robertson and Falwell called for extensive support of the

military to defend Israel in the last battle with atheistic Russia.

Mixing on the Left

Mainline denominations also allied their religion to politics, taking stands on such issues as racial integration, disarmament, cleaning up the environment, aid to the poor, and peace through justice.

As a teenager, I remember hearing sermons condemning a man called Rauschenbush for his Social Gospel. I had no idea what that meant, but I suspected that it was of the devil and would probably destroy the church. Later in Seminary, when I learned about Walter Rauschenbush, I was confused. He did not seem like such a bad man to me. He looked at the poor living in slums, working in sweatshops, watching their children die for lack of health care and often turning to crime, and he wanted to help. Advocates of the Social Gospel preached against a view of sin as private and mainly sexual, while all around them were the poor and oppressed. Rauschenbush was convinced that the limited charities of the church could never address the vastness of slums and sweatshops. Problems of this size required political action.

It was in the same tradition that Martin Luther King, Jr. organized the Montgomery bus boycott to combat the evils of racism. Someone said, "If I feed the hungry, they call me a saint. If I ask why they are hungry, they call me a communist." Some churches actually labeled King a Communist and lawbreaker, but others, in the name of the Gospel, joined him in his struggle for justice.

Christian Left theology calls for the church to work for the Kingdom of God here and now on earth. To witness to the Kingdom requires that we work for God's will to be "done on earth as it is in heaven." God is always concerned for the poor. Most social problems are political problems and cannot be solved by individual piety. Christians must fight social evils in the political arena.

Christianity demands justice, therefore it will never be possible to separate religion from politics. The wall is a myth.

How easy to identify the interest and values of our nation with the will of God. But politics is not an avoidable evil. It's the medium through which our religious values become operational, through which we promote peace and justice, or tyranny and oppression. If we are Christians, we have no choice. We must work through politics for peace and justice.

Every argument used twenty-five years ago to justify the church's indifference to the plight of blacks, is still heard in religious groups today and used to justify the church's indifference to the plight of the Palestinians. My feeling is, in light of our history, problems come not because the church is not spiritual enough but *because the church is not political enough.*

Secular Humanism

Televangelists call "secular humanism" the number one enemy of God. Yet it's a noble word; it first came into use during the Renaissance to describe the re-appreciation of the human mind. It found expression in art, literature, music, architecture, and human dignity. Humanists rejoiced that we were made in the image of God. Seeing a unique value in every person, humanists stressed education, health and welfare for everyone, including the poor. Unlike those who had the tendency to treat human beings as things, the humanist cared first and foremost for people. The Psalmist spoke for the humanist when he said:

> When I look at thy heavens, the works of thy fingers, the moon and the stars which thou hast established; what is man, that thou art mindful of him and the son of man that thou visitest him? Yet, thou hast made him a little less than God, and dost crown him with glory and honor." (Psalm 8:3-5)

When we consider how much more we know about the universe today than the Psalmist knew, the question and its answer are far more astonishing. How could God, the creator, possibly be concerned about us? Yet Jesus told us that "even the hairs of our head are all numbered." (Matt. 10:30) God knows even the smallest detail of our being, for we are important "from the least of them to the greatest," as the New Covenant says. (Hebrews 8:11) That's humanism, the recognition of the unique worth of every human being. It is also very Christian.

That which distinguishes the Christian God from all the other gods of the world is the revelation of the humanistic nature of God in Jesus Christ. Jesus is precious to us, not so much because he believed in God like no one else ever has, but because he believed in human beings like no one else ever has. Over and over, he saw qualities of faith and love in the ordinary people that others missed. He treated his friends with dignity, his enemies with love, and the masses of people with caring concern. Jesus believed in people. The Bible with its concern for the needs and dignity of all people is a humanistic book.

Forty percent of those who live in my community, right in the heart of Bible-belt Georgia, claim no relationship to any church or synagogue. Yet many of them believe in and support human dignity. They would call themselves secular humanists; they maintain the Christian ethic without the title of religion. Fundamentalists have portrayed our secular humanist neighbors as "the enemies of God"!

So, where do Christians fit into all this? We serve God best, not by launching a head-on attack against secular humanism as some kind of twentieth-century Beelzebub, but by making a clear and loving proclamation of a humanism rooted and sustained by faith in the God of Jesus Christ. We might call it a "holy humanism," which affirms the strength and guidance we receive from the Spirit of God and the Bible. I don't want to say to the secular humanist, "Be gone, you enemy." I want to say, "Whatever your motive, your heart is right." *Our real enemy is not the secular humanist, but the inhumanist...secular or religious.* Anyone who treats human beings as things to be manipulated, used, degraded or tortured is not a friend to God. Faith in a loving God offers us a motive for loving many of those whom power and politics declare unlovely and worthless. The Christian has been given orders to seek peace, to feed the hungry, clothe the naked, and visit the sick. In other words, we are called to be humanists. Humanism is our God-given mandate.

Secular or Biblical, whatever it's called, humanists enter the battle on the side of the poor, the oppressed, the disadvantaged and the stranger. Christians find their clearest expression of humanism in what has come to be called Liberation Theology.

Chapter Five

LIBERATION THEOLOGY
AND THE STATE OF ISRAEL

The greatest threat to religion in America today is not atheism or secularism, but religion as presently portrayed. I sometimes imagine going into the streets with a microphone, saying, "I am from the church and I want to know what you mean by the word *religion*." "Well, stupid, everybody knows that. It has to do with sin and life after death."

Another would say, "It has to do with... you know, with the supernatural and things like that."

"Right. It's miracles and all..." another adds.

Many of us contrast "religion" which focuses on the other world— priests, stained glass windows, and Bach chorals— with the "secular" world of jobs, politics, and governmental elections. "Religion may be important," they say, "but it's sort of irrelevant." It's to be honored...but like the party out of power. Religion just doesn't fit into what's happening now. The prophet Amos addressed this preoccupation with otherworldly religiosity when he said:

> I hate, I despise your feasts,and I take no delight in your solemn assemblies. Even though you offer me your burnt offerings and cereal offerings, I will not accept them, and the peace offerings of your fatted beasts I will not look upon. Take away from me the noise of your songs; to the melody of your harps I will not listen. But let justice roll down like waters, and righteousness like an ever-flowing stream." (Amos 5:21-24)

Amos wanted to abolish religiosity. Its blind emphasis on ceremonies required little responsibility for such things as peace and justice. When we fail to see God in humanity, we are looking for God too high up. God inevitably commits to the side of the poor, the oppressed, and the disadvantaged.

LATIN AMERICAN LIBERATION THEOLOGY

I first encountered Liberation Theology while visiting a missionary friend in Ecuador in 1979. It was my first experience with a population of poor people. My friend, Bob Armistead, a good ol' boy from Tennessee, introduced me to a whole new arena of Christian concern. His identity with the poor people of Quito was an eye-opener for me. Often, he was the only "Gringo" crowding onto one of those public lorries designed to carry fifteen people, in which twice that many sat, stood, and clung to. He walked the crowded alleys of colonial Quito delivering medicine, seeking someone to help, or listening to stories of need. He ate food from a sidewalk vendor which turned my stomach. "If you are going to relate to them," he said, "you eat what they eat."

This matter of solidarity with the disinherited was new to me and very confusing. But listening to Bob, it seemed right... and Biblical. "To set at liberty those who are oppressed" (Luke 4:18) flashed through my mind. "How did it get started, this identity with the oppressed?" I asked. And there in the crowded slums of Quito, I got my first lesson in Liberation Theology.

Since the third century, when Constantine made Christianity the religion of Rome, the church has struggled with the cross-pull of being supported by the rich and being called of God to a concern for the poor. Especially in the past century in Latin America where the gap between rich and poor has increasingly widened, being in the church has become confusing. Surrounded by social upheavals, many priests saw their religious responsibility as baptizing the poor while serving and living like the privileged. Priests maintained a ritualistic relationship with the lower classes which were crowded elbow to elbow into slums. Clergy had learned in seminary that in some mysterious way, God was using their sacramental actions to save the lost souls of the oppressed for heaven later, while the rich and privileged exploited their bodies now. The church concentrated its efforts on building schools to serve the upper class, which could afford tuition. They wanted to provide future leaders with a "religious foundation."

To the poor, the church preached "resignation to God's will," implying that the disposition of wealth and station in life was assigned by God. "Blessed are the poor in spirit."(Matthew 5:3) "Be patient, you will get your reward in heaven," they preached. In the meantime, even those priests who took vows of poverty enjoyed a standard of living far beyond the reach of the daily agony of the laboring poor. Peasants mostly saw priests as a part of the unjust social order. Everyone, priests and parishioners alike, felt the tensions.

Medellin: Liberation Theology Takes Shape

On August, 1968, 130 Roman Catholic bishops, representing more than 600 priests, met in Medellin, Colombia to struggle with the tension between the image and the call of priesthood. How does one live with the rich and minister to the poor? Medellin became the "Rubicon" for a new theology which had flooded the world church. The bishops called for Christians to transform society and denounce "institutionalized violence." They expanded the traditional notion of sin which focused on individual transgressions against religious laws, and identified systematic abuses of human rights as being not just social concerns, but sins against the will of God. They called for the church to share in the condition of the marginalized masses and *to give preferential treatment to the poor through solidarity.* These bishops frequently used the term "liberation" as a goal of lifting the masses of people from "less human to more human conditions." Medellin became the Magna Carta for the role of the church and a new approach to pastoral ministry.

One of the most influential framers of the Theology of Liberation is Gustavo Gutierrez. This Peruvian priest moved theology from the classrooms to the streets. The social context of Latin America required a new theology, he said. In North America, Christian theology embraced a rich world. Its major concern was to defend Christianity's credibility. How could a modern, scientific-minded congregation believe in a God who walks on water, parts the seas, multiplies loaves, and raises people from the dead? While North American theologians were trying the sort out the different levels of meanings to Biblical stories, theologians in South America faced a different question. The masses were not asking if Christianity was true, but rather *was Christianity relevant to their struggle for a just world?* They asked, "How can anyone be tortured or murdered in the name of God?" To them, the God question was not whether God exists, but what kind of God is God?

According to Gutierrez, poverty is the starting place for theology, for God is involved in the struggle of oppressed people for liberation. Gutierrez took the position that poverty is man-made. Poverty is an evil and is against the will of God. The Bible says, "He was rich, yet for your sake he became poor, so that through his poverty, you might become rich." (II Corinthians 8:9) The church is called to the same kind of solidarity with the poor, in order that its true spirituality might find fulfillment.

Eleven years after Medellin, in 1979, the Latin American bishops meeting in Puebla, Mexico reaffirmed their commitment to Medellin, saying:

> We see the growing gap between rich and poor as a scandal and a contradiction to Christian existence. The luxury of a few becomes an insult to the wretched poverty of the vast masses...[1]

Opposition to Medellin

Since the beginning of time, Government (including the military), Religion (including the church), and Business have been in bed together. They co-habit. They have looked after each others' needs and lined each others' pockets. Leaders of the church have enjoyed the financial benefits of economically strong states while offering "God's blessings" upon their military battles. Of course, there have been exceptions, such as Saint Frances and Albert Schweitzer, but for the most part, the established church has identified with the rich and powerful.

Medellin believed that resolution could come through a change of heart on the part of the privileged and powerful and called for a "conversion of the baptized." Surely the bias of God for the poor and oppressed would overcome the greed of the rich and powerful. Surely those best educated and most blessed would hear the Gospel of liberation for the "least of these" and support the social concerns of the priests.

But that did not happen. Shifting the emphasis from personal salvation to correcting the injustices in society led to the murder of dozens of priests and thousands of lay people. Every day brought new reports of arrests, beatings, torture and intimidation. Between 1964 and 1978, 41 priests were killed, 11 disappeared, 485 were arrested, 46 tortured, and 253 expelled.[2]

The priesthood of the church was no longer identified with the elite and once again, like during the New Testament period, the church was experiencing large numbers of martyrs. Most famous of those who became victims of the opposition to Liberation Theology was Archbishop Oscar Romero of El Salvador. Romero had been chosen by Rome to bring the church back into the fold, to re-establish its marriage to the empire. But when Romero witnessed the oppression of the poor, he changed. The month he was killed, March, 1980, Amnesty International attested that 83 people had been killed by right wing military forces in four days. On March 24, while serving mass, Oscar Romero was assassinated while he was telling soldiers to disobey orders:

> My brothers, they are part of our very own people. You are killing your own fellow peasants. God's law, "Thou shalt not kill," takes precedence over a human being's order to kill. No soldier is obligated to obey an order that is against God's law. No one has to obey an immoral law.[3]

The gospel of liberation is never welcomed by power. Such resistance by the upper class was inevitable, considering the nature of power. Our patterns of conduct demonstrate that most often, the more power we have, the less concerned we are for justice. God might unite power and love for justice, but humans, given enough power, begin to think of themselves as little gods, above such things as justice. Those in power make, interpret, and enforce the laws in favor of those in power. Justice is conceived by the ruling class in such a way as to sustain the privileges of the elite. What is good for the powerful is seen as right and becomes law. Torture, killings, collective punishment, detentions,intimidations, and beatings are justified because it is the law...of the powerful.

In this context, liberation theologians see in Jesus Christ the human fulfillment of service to others. He turned the empire's marks of success up-side down. "Blessed are you poor," he said, and "woe to you rich". (Luke 6:20,24) Jesus invited the poor and outcast to the banquet, and leveled harsh criticism on the elite, the rich, the priests, and rulers.

Liberation theologians realize the opposition they will encounter from the state, which will fight any change of the status quo. Liberation Theology reads the words of Jesus to "take up your cross" as a call to a willingness to die.

The Reagan administration countered the effects of Liberation Theology by accusing liberation theologians of using the church as a political weapon against private property and productive capitalism. The religious community was accused of being infiltrated with communist ideas.Yet, some strange and unexpected results have been recorded in the church.

Liberation Theology Revitalizes the Church

Those of us who are protestants should note that much of our Reformed Theology grew out of a small radius in central Europe, namely Germany and Switzerland. Our fathers in faith have German names: Bultmann, Brunner, Tillich, Barth, and two Neibuhrs. Most Reformed theologians stressed those things that a Christian must believe about Jesus, such as the virgin birth, the resurrection, and the second coming.

It seems significant that today, 300 years after the Reformation, the protestant churches in the heart of reformation territory are mostly empty. Few large gatherings of people crowd into the churches of Germany and Switzerland today except for an organ recital or funeral. The influence of the church is hardly noticeable to the average person on the street. On the other hand, in Latin America, the church has committed itself to Liberation Theology with an emphasis not on believing certain things *about* Jesus, but on believing *in* Jesus. It seeks to follow his life-style. And we find the church growing faster than we can count. In Central and South America alone, there are 70,000 base community churches meeting in homes, studying the Bible, claiming two and a half million members.

Liberation Theology begins with the poor and then works out its theology. The poor claim a relationship with God that the rich seldom know. In the context of death squads murdering hundreds of citizens every year, churches whose members are subject to torture, expulsion and prison are taking a stand against violence, and they are growing. Their theology and their numbers grow out of action.

According to Gutierrez, theology is always the second step, growing out of involvement in life. Faith cannot be neutral. "If you are neutral in a situation of injustice, you have chosen the side of the oppressor," says Desmond Tutu. In other words, not to act is to act. To the liberation theologian, commitment comes first. Then in the midst of the struggle for justice, Biblical reflection gives form to a *theology based on meeting human needs.*

Of course, the rich and powerful think of Liberation Theology as dirty pool. "You are taking sides," they say. "Religion and politics don't mix." Yet for years, while the church took the side of the elite and endorsed their control of society, the rich never complained about the mixture of religion and politics. The truth is, the church is not taking sides for the first time. What disturbs the elite is that the church is *changing* sides and the masses of people are becoming a part of it. In reality, liberation theologians are simply taking a new look at some old familiar Biblical themes.

Liberation theologians see the story of Adam and Eve as God's creating people in his own image and pronouncing them all "good." Thus, abuse of a human being denies God's good creation and commits a sin. Torture is not just a sin against the victim; torture mocks God. The sin of Cain was not just the murder of Abel but Cain's refusal to care for his brother. The consequences of his sin were that he no longer had a brother to care for and was banished to live alone. Thus, solidarity with our brother is the only hope of Godly life.

In the third world, Jesus is not dead or mute, represented on a cross, but alive and involved in the struggle for justice. Liberation Theology focuses on Jesus' life and message. His first sermon:

"The Spirit of the Lord is upon me, because he has anointed me to preach good news to the poor. He has sent me to proclaim release to the captives, and recovering of sight to the blind, to set at liberty those who are oppressed, to proclaim the acceptable year of the Lord." (Luke 4:18-19)

His last sermon:

"Come, O blessed of my father, inherit the kingdom prepared for you from the foundation of the world; for I was hungry and you gave me food, I was thirsty and you gave me drink, I was a stranger and you welcomed me, I was naked and you clothed me, I was sick and you visited me, I was in prison and you came to me." Then the righteous will answer him, "Lord, when did we see thee hungry and feed thee, or thirsty and give thee drink? And when did we see thee a stranger and welcome thee, or naked and clothe thee? And when did we see thee sick or in prison and visit thee?" And the King will answer them, "Truly, I say to you, as you did it to one of the least of these my brethren, you did it unto me." (Matthew 25:34-41)

LIBERATION THEOLOGY IN THE MIDDLE EAST

It would be hard to miss the significance of Liberation Theology for the people of Israel-Palestine. The social and Biblical situation addressed by the liberation theologians of Latin America parallels the political situation in Israel/Palestine today. Oppressed people learn to read the Bible in a way that affirms their dignity and self-worth and their right to struggle for a more decent life.

The Exodus Story: God Takes Sides

The defenders of Israel's policies toward the Palestinians love the Exodus story. "God gave this land to us," they quote, "and the Palestinians just have to accept it. This is our land. They must move out or suffer the consequences." But if the Exodus narrative is to be taken seriously, then we should also look at the Exodus account through the eyes of the Liberation Theologian, such as Robert McAfee Brown, who in *Unexpected News*[4] unpacks the Exodus story as seen through the eyes of the third world reader.

The Biblical text reads:

Now there arose a new king over Egypt, who did not know Joseph. And he said to his people, "Behold, the people of Israel are too many and too mighty for us. Come, let us deal shrewdly with them, lest they multiply, and, if war befall us, they join our enemies and fight against us and escape from the land." Therefore they set taskmasters over them to afflict them with heavy burdens; and they built for Pharaoh story-cities, Pithom and Raamses. But the more they were oppressed, the more they spread abroad. And the Egyptians were in dread of the people of Israel. So they made the people of Israel serve with rigor, and made their lives bitter with hard service, in mortar and brick, and in all kinds of work in the field; in all their work they made them serve with rigor.(Exodus 1:8-14)

In the course of those many days the king died. And the people of Israel groaned under the bondage, and cried out for help, and their cry under bondage came up to God. And God saw the people of Israel, and God knew their condition. (Exodus 2:23-25)

Then the Lord said, "I have seen the affliction of my people who are in Egypt, and have heard their cry because of their taskmasters; I know their sufferings, and I have come down to deliver them out of the hand of the Egyptians, and to bring them up out of that land to a good and broad land; a land flowing with milk and honey, to the place of the Canaanites, the Hittites, the Amorites, the Perizzites, the Hivites, and the Jebusites. And now, behold, the cry of the people of Israel has come to me, and I have seen the oppression with which the Egyptians oppress them. Come, I will send you to Pharaoh that you may bring forth my people, the sons of Israel out of Egypt.(Exodus 3:7-10)

This text leaves little doubt that a struggle was going on between two classes of people, oppressors and oppressed. The Israelites were slaves; the Egyptians were slavemasters. Pharaoh justified every act of oppression on the grounds of security. "Come, let us deal shrewdly with them, lest they multiply, and, if war befall us, they join our enemies and fight against us." But God was also aware of the struggle. The Israelites cried out to God and he heard their cry. God did not side with the powerful, but *with the oppressed.*

God's liberation was not a "you just wait and heaven will be yours." God's liberation was a political liberation in this world and in the present, indicating God's intention that religion and politics should mix. Then, God called the oppressed to join in the struggle. "I will send you to Pharaoh." The conquered, trusting in the power of God to deliver them, became involved in their own liberation. God did not do it without their help. They had to act out of their own determination not to remain powerless. Oppressors will not voluntarily relinquish power. *God did not enlighten the powerful but empowered the powerless.*

Israel apparently reads this text and sees only the words, "to a good and broad land; a land flowing with milk and honey, to the place of the Canaanites." But to see only a gift of real estate requires a gross blindness to the rest of the text. In today's world, any honest reader would identify, not the State of Israel, but the Palestinians, as the oppressed. Palestinians realize that they are the oppressed. Awareness of oppression is not something gleaned from books; it's a gnawing hunger in the gut. It's a father taken off at 2 A.M. to face torture and death, children growing up in the squalor of a refugee camp, family members hauled off to prison without trial. It's being victimized by beatings, breaking of bones, and killings. It's seeing your homeland confiscated by a powerful Pharaoh, and realizing that your future is likely to be lived in unredeemed poverty while the oppressor lives in what seems like unimagined opulence.

But for the oppressed, according to Robert McAfee Brown:

> There is good news. They are not alone. God is aware of the struggle they face. God always sides with the oppressed. A God who sided with no one is indifferent, giving support to the tyrants by not opposing them.[5]

Christians have to admit that the Palestinians, including Muslims, may have a legitimate interpretation of the Exodus story, one closer to the Gospel than that of the Zionists. And if that is so, many comfortable middle-class Christians are on the wrong side of the struggle.

Biblical Principles Missed by Israel

Many great themes run throughout the scriptures of the Old and New testaments. Some would say personal salvation. Others would identify piety or mystical experiences or miracles. The apostle Paul lifted up faith, hope, and love. I would not argue with any of these and would add monotheism, grace, discipleship and worship. But most of all, I would include the theme of *justice.*

The peace which stands the test of scripture lifts out some important distinctions between the teachings of the Bible and the current practice of Israel. The difference between Biblical Israel and the current state is seen in how differently the Biblical writers and modern Israel see the matters of peace, justice, the land, and the concept of chosenness.

1 - PEACE

In Rome nearly 2000 years ago, Caesar Augustus claimed to be the Prince of Peace. He had accomplished his victories by military force. He conquered his rivals and imposed peace by power. Into his world came Jesus of Nazareth announcing another kind of peace, a peace founded on justice and compassion. The conflict that followed culminated in the crucifixion of Jesus by the followers of Augustus, and the struggle between these two ways of peace continues to this day.

Where in the world did we get the idea that true peace could ever come from force? Some claim that force is justified in the Bible, quoting some very bloodthirsty passages in the Old Testament, such as the Psalmist saying, "Happy shall he be who takes your little ones and dashes them against the rock." (Psalm 137:9) Or when King Saul was condemned for not following divine orders to "go and smite Amalek, and utterly destroy all that they have; do not spare them, but kill both man and woman, infant and suckling, ox and sheep, camel and ass." (I Samuel 15:3) In several places the God of the Old Testament seems to employ warfare to accomplish his political goals.

On the other hand, Jesus rebuked Peter, who pulled his sword, saying, "All who take the sword will perish by the sword." (Matt. 26:52) Jesus calls upon us to love and pray for our enemies. All through the Bible, we read of God's love for all people and God's ultimate commitment to peace:

> They shall beat the swords into plowshares, and their spears into pruning hooks. Nation shall not lift up sword against nation, neither shall they learn war any more. (Isaiah 2:4)

The apostle Paul, quoting the Old Testament wrote to the Corinthians:

> For the whole law is fulfilled in one word. 'You shall love your neighbor as yourself." (Gal. 5:14)

Jesus, when asked to summarize the law, responded:

> You shall love the Lord your God with all your heart, and with all your soul, and with all your mind. This is the great

and first commandment. And a second is like it, You shall love your neighbor as yourself. (Matthew 22:37-38)

In his sermon on the mount, Jesus did not offer praise to the warrior, but said "Blessed are the peacemakers."

2 - JUSTICE

An examination of the Old Testament (the Jewish Scriptures) confirms that peace is not passive, but has a direct relationship with justice. These are two sides of the same coin. According to Israel's own theology, there can be *no peace without justice.*

Today, when I hear the Hebrew word "Shalom," my soul is jabbed by the awareness that this is the "good morning" of the Israeli soldier. It is the greeting of those who come in the night to arrest and imprison without charge, to separate children from their parents, to convict by "secret evidence" on confessions obtained by torture, who shoot, beat and kill, and who lock up human beings in camps hardly fit for animals. What a prostitute shalom has become. If shalom is to regain integrity, it must defend justice. Robert McAfee Brown puts it simply, "Whatever is unjust threatens peace."

If my children were hungry when food was available, I would probably become violent. If an Israeli soldier took my land, abused members of my family, threatened me and treated me as a non-person, I would find some way to fight back. Even if they kill me, my friends would take up the cause and my death would add to the flame of violence. Belief in a God of justice generates anger toward the practice of injustice. It's not a hatred, but an anger that energizes peaceloving people to work for justice.

Peace does not come cheap or easy. We must learn to discern between true peace and false peace. One is the peace of the strong and the powerful. It's the peace of the status quo. It seeks to maintain everything as it is. It says, "Don't rock the boat. Don't disturb the peace." Such a passive peace is a fake peace. It describes itself in negative terms: no fighting, no shooting, no demonstrations, no problems.

On the other hand, genuine peace is the peace brought about by achieving justice for the weak and oppressed. It calls for change to overcome evil. It is a positive peace. It talks about building, creating, moving ahead, doing something about unjust structures and changing the systems.

One is a peace of passivity. It's the peace of the dead, or of the imprisoned, those who have been silenced. It's a peace enforced by power. The other is a peace brought about by justice. When we talk about peace without justice in the same breath, it's false.

One is a temporary peace, the other is a lasting peace.

One is a peace of appearances. It looks good on the outside. The other is a peace of substance and reality.

One shoves problems under the rug. It hides from all difficult issues. It just wants things under control. The other wrestles with hard issues until it finds solutions.

The battle between Christ and Augustus is not finished. Peacemakers are called to work for genuine peace.

3 - LAND

Another principle missed by modern Israel involves the Biblical principle of land ownership - the land belongs to God. Although modern Israel has unashamedly declared itself a secular state, Cabinet Ministers quote from the Old Testament to justify Israel's claim to the captured territories. Golda Meir, while claiming to be personally non-religious, once said, "This country exists as a result of a promise made by God Himself." Prime Minister Shamir insisted on referring to the captured territories as Samaria and Judea. He hoped to confuse American fundamentalist Christians into believing that there is a connection between Biblical Israel, those through whom all the families of the earth are to be blessed, and the present state of Israel.

Modern Israel lays claim to the occupied territories on the basis of God's promise to Abraham:

> On that day the Lord made a covenant with Abram, saying, "To your descendents I give this land, from the river of Egypt to the great river, the river of Euphrates..." (Genesis 15:18)

Yet modern Israel shows little interest in the Biblical responsibility that comes with that promise. It's fascinating how consistently the promise of land to Israel is tied to the responsibility of being a blessing to all nations:

... I will make of you a great nation, and I will bless you, and make your name great, so that you will be a blessing. I will bless those who bless you, and him who curses you I will curse; and by you all the families of the earth shall bless themselves." (Genesis 12:2-3)

...I will multiply your descendants as the stars of heaven, and I will give to your descendents all these lands; and by your descendents all the nations of the earth shall bless themselves. (Genesis 26:4)

...and your descendants shall be like the dust of the earth, and you shall spread abroad to the west and to the east and to the north and to the south; and by you and your descendants shall all the families of the earth bless themselves. (Genesis 28:14)

...I will indeed bless you, and I will multiply your descendents as the stars of heaven and as the sand which is on the seashore. And your descendents shall possess the gate of their enemies, and by your descendents shall all the nations of the earth bless themselves, because you have obeyed my voice. (Genesis 22:17-18)

According to the Jewish scriptures, there is no doubt that Yahweh gave land to Israel. But the same scriptures which provide rights to the land also, and just as consistently, *connect the gift of land to the responsibility to bless the nations of the world.*

It is also significant to note that Abraham bought the land. Colin Chapman, in *Whose Promised Land*, says:

> Abraham didn't actually own any piece of land until his wife Sarah died many years after. And it's strange that one whole chapter of Genesis is devoted to Abraham's negotiations for the purchase of the cave in Hebron where he buried his wife. But these details begin to make sense when we see that this marked the very first stage of the fulfillment of God's promises. Abraham didn't assume that God's promise about the land gave him the right to steal it from its current owners. And he wasn't interested in accepting the cave as a gift. He insisted on buying the land, paying its full value and making legal contract in the presence of witnesses.[6]

I ask if an alleged promise made to a wandering shepherd nearly 4000 years ago and not recorded until 800 years later in a book accepted as "from God" by only a fraction of the world's population should hold such ultimate authority for so much pain and power and indeed, be expanded to include actions beyond its apparent purview? *Ha'aretz*, one of the leading newspapers of Israel, quotes a Rabbi of captain rank as justifying the 1982 invasion and massacre of Lebanon:

> We must not overlook the Biblical sources which justify this war (the 1982 war in Lebanon) and our presence here. We are fulfilling our religious duty as Jews by being here. So it is written: the religious duty to conquer the Land from the enemy.[7]

It is significant that Ishmael is also a son of Abraham. In order to continue the family line when Sarah proved barren, Abraham, following the custom of his day, had a child by Hagar, Sarah's Egyptian maid. Thus many Arabs today will claim that as the sons of Abraham, Arabs have an equal right to "Eretz Israel" because of the promises to Ishmael. According to many Arab scholars of the Bible, the promise made "To your descendants" (Genesis 12:7 and 15:18) is clarified when God says to Abraham:

> And I will make a nation of the son of the slave woman also, because he is your offspring. (Genesis 21:13)

In fact, when the covenant promise of land was originally made with Abraham, it was Ishmael who was circumcised. Isaac had not yet been born.

There are some scholars (and a part of me), who say that the Biblical accounts of God's giving land to Israel are made up by the ancient Hebrews to justify their brutal occupation of the land. How ironic that in the 20th Century, this tactic should be used once again. The Zionist claims to ownership of Palestine are based on a very selective and self-serving reading of the Old Testament. The claim of the Jewish scriptures that the land belongs to Jews only holds little authority for Christian and Muslim Arabs.

The Earth is the Lord's

The land always has and always will belong to God. Even according to Jewish scriptures:

...the land is mine and you are but aliens and my tenants. (Leviticus 25:23)

... the earth is the Lord's and the fullness thereof, the world and those who dwell therein. (Psalm 24:1)

The giving of the land to Israel cannot be seen as an end in itself. It is but one stage in the unfolding drama of God's universal love for all people. Along with the gift of land came a warning that if Israel failed in God's purpose to bless all nations, Israel itself would be expelled from the land.

But you shall keep my statutes and my ordinances and do none of these abominations, either the native or the stranger who sojourns among you (for all of those abominations the men of the land did, who were before you, so that the land became defiled); lest the land vomit you out, when you defile it, as it vomited out the nation that was before you. (Leviticus 18:26-28)

Beware lest you say in your heart, "My power and the might of my hand have gotten me this wealth." You shall remember the Lord your God, for it is he who gives you power to get wealth; that he may confirm his covenant which he swore to your fathers, as at this day. And if you forget the Lord your God and go after other gods and serve them and worship them, I solemnly warn you this day that you shall surely perish. (Deuteronomy 8:17-19)

God gave the land as a responsibility. This gift could be withdrawn if the people were disobedient.

More than once, ancient Israel, God's chosen people, was shocked to be exiled from the land. The land was a gift but it carried with it an obligation to obey the law of God. The assumption of a perpetual right to the land fell apart when Nebuchadnezzar drove the Jews from the land in 597 B.C., forcing them to live as refugees in Babylon. Later, in 70 A.D., Rome drove Israel into an exile from which it did not return for nearly 1900 years.

Can modern Israel not realize that to exploit God's will for justice for all people could lead to another expulsion? Moses warned the Israelites before entering the promised land:

> When you beget children and children's children, and have grown old in the land if you act corruptly by making a graven image in the form of any thing, and by doing what is evil in the sight of the Lord your God, so as to provoke him to anger, I call heaven and earth to witness against you this day, that you will soon utterly perish from the land which you are going over the Jordan to possess; you will not live long upon it, but it will utterly be destroyed. And the Lord will scatter you among the people, and you will be left in number among the nations where the Lord will drive you. (Deuteronomy 4:25-27)

Again:

> But if you turn aside from following me, you or your children, and do not keep my commandments and my statutes which I have set before you, but go and serve other gods and worship them, then I will cut off Israel from the land which I have given them. (I Kings 9:6-7)

In short, modern Zionists overlook a very significant condition for the land they claim God gave to them: possession of the land is conditioned on obedience to the will of God to bless all people.

Land Does Not Represent the Heart of God's Gift

Naturally Christians (or Muslims or secularists) are not limited to the Old Testament to direct their understanding of Israel. Christians should recall that the New Testament places no significance in the land as such, not even Jerusalem, other than its being the birth place of Jesus. The great commission of our Lord to the early church lets us know that in the mind of Jesus, the establishment of the modern state of Israel has no significance for the kingdom of God. His is a spiritual kingdom for the whole earth, with no connection to any one political state.

> ...and you shall be my witnesses in Jerusalem and in all Judea and Samaria and to the end of the earth. (Acts1:8)

The New Testament gives a new meaning to the concept of "inheritance."

> Blessed be the God and father of our Lord Jesus Christ! By his great mercy we have been born anew to a living hope through the resurrection of Jesus Christ from the dead, and to an inheritance which is imperishable, undefiled, and unfading, kept in heaven for you. (I Peter 1:3-4)

Peter speaks of another inheritance which has no reference to the land, but to the kingdom of God. It includes not just the biological descendents of Abraham but all the faithful people of God. As far as we know, Paul never mentioned the land. He believed that Jesus was the fulfillment of all the divine promises, which includes all people.

> For in Christ Jesus you are all sons of God, through faith. For as many of you as were baptized into Christ have put on Christ. There is neither Jew nor Greek, there is neither slave nor free, there is neither male nor female; for you are all one in Christ Jesus. And if you are Christ's, then you are Abraham's offspring, heirs according to promise. (Galatians 3:26-29)

In this text, the name *Israel includes all races and people who recognize Jesus as the Messiah.* Paul goes on to say:

> For neither circumcision counts for anything, nor uncircumcision, but a new creation. (Galatians 6:15)

Thus, *the Jews are no longer in exclusive possession of the call to be Israel.* Christians believe that the temple and its sacrifices have been fulfilled once and for all in Jesus Christ. Christians should remember that:

- Jesus never mentioned the land except to predict the destruction of Jerusalem.

- Jesus himself is the fulfillment of all the promises made to Abraham.

- The life, death, and resurrection of Jesus Christ accomplished the "redemption" of "Israel" and has nothing to do with land.

4 - CHOSENNESS

The fourth biblical principle missed by the modern state of Israel involves its faithfulness to the call of chosenness.

Deuteronomy says:

> And now Israel, what does the Lord your God require of you, but to fear the Lord your God, to walk in all his ways, to love him, to serve the Lord your God with all your heart and with all your soul, and to keep the commandments and statutes of the Lord, which I command you this day for your good? Behold, to the Lord your God belongs the heaven and the heaven of heavens, the earth with all that is in it; yet, the Lord set his heart in love upon your fathers and chose their descendents after them, you above all peoples, as at this day. Circumcise therefore the foreskin of your heart, and be no longer stubborn. For the Lord your God is God of gods and Lord of lords, the great, the almighty, and the terrible God, who is not partial and takes no bribes. He executes justice for the fatherless and the widow, and loves the sojouner, giving him food and clothing. Love the sojourner therefore; for you were sojourners in the land of Egypt. (Deuteronomy 10:12-13)

This text spells out five requirements. Israel should (1) reverence, love and fear God. She shall (2) serve God, (3) keep his commandments, (4) dedicate (circumcise) the heart and (5) love the stranger. That's it. Not one word about status. Israel is to be responsible. God is impartial. He did not choose Israel for special privilege, but for service. Israel is called of God to emulate God in caring for the needy in society. She has an obligation to the poor and the weak because of her own past experience in Egypt. The affluent who have been poor have special responsibility not to despise the poor.

It is significant that Israel is called to circumcise the heart. True Judaism is not a nationalism, but a love for God and is humble submission to his universal will. Deuteronomy says:

> You shall not pervert justice; you shall not show partiality; and you shall not take a bribe, for a bribe blinds the eyes of the wise and perverts the cause of the righteous. Justice, and only justice you shall follow, that you may live and inherit the land which the Lord your God gives you. (Deuteronomy 16:19-20)

The writer of Deuteronomy never forgets the welfare of the disempowered. He condemns the use of bribes to pervert justice.

91

> The father shall not be put to death for the children, nor shall the children be put to death for the fathers; every man shall be put to death for his own sin. You shall not pervert the justice due the sojourner or to the fatherless, or take a widow's garment in pledge; but you shall remember that you were slaves in Egypt and the Lord your God redeemed you from there. (Deuteronomy24:16-17)

This text is concerned with the protection of the underprivileged, especially the sojourner. Many foreigners came to Israel because of debt, injustice or oppression. They were poor and were ready targets for prejudice, ill-treatment and all manner of social injustice at the hands of the well-armed Israelites. Deuteronomy was written to protect such people. It reinforces the older law that protected a family from sharing the penalty imposed on one particular member of it who had committed a crime.

SOLIDARITY WITH THE PALESTINIANS

In the context of this book, the question is: where is God in the Israeli\Palestinian conflict? That answer is, as always, God is on the side of the oppressed.

What has happened to "do justly, love mercy, and walk humbly?" All this has been sold out for "do expediently, love power and triumph arrogantly over thy neighbor," or anyone who gets in the way of Israeli expansionism. The essence of the Israeli state is expansion, not religion. But when the Jewish state makes expendable the indigenous Palestinian culture and community in historic Palestine, when it is bent on eliminating the Palestinians people in historic Palestine, then to quote Marc Ellis:

> At this juncture, Israel is an anti-Jewish power committed to land and dominance, in which case, Israel will survive as long, and only as long, as it maintains sufficient power to force its will on the rest of the world. This, to many, both inside and outside Israel, seems to be a path toward destruction. Sooner or later, like all Empires, Israel will lose a war, and will be destroyed.[8]

Compassion is the very fabric of Judaism. Thus, Robert McAfee Brown makes a plea to Israel:

You, more than all the other peoples on earth, know what it is like to be refugees, sojourners, displaced persons, people whose lands have been overrun time and again by invaders. Your Psalms and liturgies invoke that sense of homelessness as something to be overcome. The Torah calls on you to welcome the sojourner, to feed the hungry, to care for the sick and dying. Could you not exercise that kind of concern for the Palestinians within your gates?[9]

Modern Israel's own past experience should lead Israel, of all people, to bear responsibility for the lot of the underprivileged. In view of the policies of the modern state of Israel and the call of God to the Biblical Israel to be a nation through whom all the nations of the earth shall be blessed, it is clear: *Israel is not Israel.*

None of us woke up today seeking someone to oppress, but we can understand if a Palestinian mother considers the American government among the oppressors. As ordinary citizens, we don't make the big political decisions, but we acquiesce in them. We don't torture people, but our tax money finances the training of those who do. We don't enforce Israel's policies, but we are complacent in our government's decisions to offer blind support. So the question is: do we end up among the oppressors by default?

Everybody wants peace. We would even be willing to work for peace if we just knew what to do, we say. Pope Paul VI (or Reinhold Neibuhr, I have seen both credited) answers, *"If you want peace, work for justice."*

Chapter Six

HOW ISRAEL INFLUENCES AMERICA

It goes like this.

"Senator, we are ready to mail out a few checks. Some have your name on 'em and they add up to four figures. We hope they will help out in your coming re-election bid."

"Thank you," the senator responds. "I am grateful for your support."

"You should be hearing from us soon, probably within the week. By the way Senator, you know we have this bill coming up and we... well we hope you will be able to see it our way. We will be very interested in how you vote. We will try to get those checks in the mail to you right away."

Many legislators swear that they are not influenced by such conversations. "I just vote my conscience," they say. Others, looking at the voting record of our legislators and the special interest groups who support them, would call it "Votes for sale." Former Senator James G. Abourezk says:

> The Israeli lobby in the United States has found the political erogenous zone of most congressional candidates - money - and applies pressure on that zone very effectively. Because most politicians care very little for either Arabs or Jews, it becomes for them simply a matter of who can contribute the most money to their campaigns.[1]

Other lobbies pale before the light of the Jewish lobby. Some call it the most effective and vicious in Washington. It makes an art out of the techniques of putting pressure on members of Congress, not for the benefit of the people of America, but for Israel. Its main concern is military and economic aid, and it pays off. During the 1988 election cycle, pro-Israel PACs (Political Action Committees) spent $5,432,055 on congressional campaigns ($6.9 million in 1986) during which time Israel received over six *billion* in direct grants, paid for by U.S. taxpayers.[2] That's over $1,100 for each dollar spent lobbying Congress for aid.

In 1980, Stephen Solarz, anxious to help Israel at all costs, led the move to relieve Israel of its obligation to repay the $785 million in economic aid and grant a permanent free ride courtesy of the American taxpayer. In 1983, Congressman George Crockett warned that an additional increase of aid to Israel would:

> free additional capital for [Israeli Prime Minister]Begin to continue building settlements. But Kansas republican Congressman Larry Winn countered by stating that increasing the grant money would "help" Israel meet its debt service obligation to the United States, which in 1983 would top $1 billion. Winn, in affect, was arguing that the United States should give Israel money to repay its debt to the United States. That sort of "logic" prevailed.[3]

In 1986, Congress did just that by passing the Cranston Amendment which made it law that "U.S. aid to Israel shall not be less than [Israel's] annual debt repayment, interest and principle." This guarantees a spotless repayment record for Israel.

AIPAC, the American Israeli Political Affairs Committee, says that it is not a Political Action Committee, that it does not make campaign contributions. But AIPAC calls the shots for about 80 pro-Israel PACs which gave over $6 million in 1988 to their candidates. That buys a lot of congressional clout. Of course, the lobby is not that obvious. Most pro-Israel PACs have rather innocuous names like National PAC, Joint Action Committee or St. Louisans for Better Government. Of the 124 pro-Israel PACs established since 1976, only six mention the Middle East, Israel, or Zionism in their title, but their commitment is none the less to Israel.

THE IMPACT OF PRO-ZIONIST PACs ON THE U.S. ELECTORAL PROCESS

Does PAC money really buy access to lawmakers? One PAC director answers:

> Oh, I don't think there's any question that it makes it easy for me to pick up the phone and get a call back. I'm not just "Bill *who?*" I'm Bill the PAC, the people who give you a good chunk of dough. We don't get a vote from 'em all the time, but we sure have the access."[4]

There is a very thin line between a PAC and a bribe. Imagine a judicial system where the defendant made regular contributions to the judge, where the court ruled, not on the basis of merit but according to who makes the largest contribution to the judge's re-election.

Politicians are quick to point out that PACs have a legal limit. No more than $5,000 to a candidate in the Primary and another $5,000 in the general election. No PAC can legally donate more than $10,000 in a single election year. What politicians don't tell about is "bundling." A mere $5,000 would be too small a part of today's election cost to "buy" much attention. But $168,000 or more would do it.

Such large amounts are achieved by bundling. Bundling skirts legal ceilings by having donors send money to a central committee that in turn distributes funds to chosen candidates, crediting the gift to the original donor. In 1988, pro-Israel PACs donated more than $5.4 million to 477 candidates. Three candidates received more than $200,000 each, four others more than $100,000.

PACs are "dirty money" designed to intimidate Congresspeople into voting for legislation which they know is not in the best interest of the United States. For this reason, the pro-Israel lobby will concentrate a quarter of a million dollars on a single campaign; that's 25 times the legal limit for a single political action committee.

Running on the Pro-Israel Ticket

According to Senate records, Bob Packwood with the help of PACs amassed $6.7 million for his 1986 campaign. According to senate records, over 95 percent of Packwood's itemized donations (those over $200) have come from out-of-state donors. Add non-itemized contributions, and some analysts estimate *as much as 98 percent of Packwood's entire reelection funds come from out of state.*

"It stinks," says attorney Harry Londale from Bend, Oregon. "The guy is supposed to represent Oregonians, but where is he getting his $3 million from? Not from us."5

And how does Mr. Packwood do it? Junk mail.

Approximately 75 percent of Packwood's donations have come from nationwide mailings primarily targeted to two groups, pro-choice Republicans and supporters of Israel's Likud government. As of June 1990, at least 1.5 million unsolicited fund-raising letters had been mailed to one million people from around the country.[6]

In his letters, Packwood predicts that Israel is on the verge of being destroyed by those who would cut aid. He wrote:

Dear friend, Please forgive the informal nature of this letter, but it is late in the evening, and my secretary already has gone home. What I want to discuss with you is Israel's future. It simply could not wait until morning.[7]

Another letter:

I share your determination to do whatever I possibly can to help guarantee Israel's security and freedom - now and forever. But to do that, I am going to need your immediate help... instead of spending all my time raising money for my own re-election campaign, I'd prefer to devote my time and energies to protecting and defending the security of Israel.[8]

I wonder if Packwood represents the people of Oregon, the government of the United States, or does he represent the government of Israel. Nick Khuory, former director of the Portland chapter of the American-Arab Anti-Discrimination Committee, said: "Packwood speaks as if he is in the Israeli senate instead of the U.S. Senate." On the other hand, American leaders who criticize Israel find themselves under attack.

The Perils of Criticizing Israel

Congressman Paul Findley, Republican from Illinois, claimed an almost perfect voting record in support of Israel. He was on record frequently criticizing Arab states and voted for all measures in Congress which authorized Israeli military and economic aid. He consistently supported causes applauded by Jews, both in America and Israel. But in spite of his near perfect pro-Israel voting record, Paul Findley in one term became "the number one enemy of Israel."[9]

In 1974, Representative Findley was asked by a constituent to help her son who had found himself in trouble in South Yemen (considered by our State Department as the most radical of the Arab States.) Findley visited Yemen and heard, for the first time in his political life, the "other side" of what he had always believed about Israel. In his own words, Findley said:

> After years on Capitol Hill, I had heard for the first time the Arab perspective, particularly on the plight of the Palestinians. I began to read about the Middle East, to talk with experts and to begin to understand the region. Gradually Arabs emerged as human beings"[10]

Findley began to ask questions about blind U.S. support of Israel. In the interest of peace, Findley decided to cross the line and visited Arafat on November 30, 1978 in Demascus. He wanted Arafat to clarify the terms under which the PLO would live at peace with Israel. Was Arafat ready to recognize Israel? Arafat's declaration was:

> The PLO will accept an independent Palestinian state of the West Bank and Gaza, with a connecting corridor, and in that circumstance will renounce any and all violent means to enlarge the territory of that state. We will give de facto recognition to the State of Israel. We would live at peace with all our neighbors.[11]

Findley was excited to hear in Arafat's words a slight hope for peace. On the other hand, AIPAC could only see a traitor in Findley. Immediately the retaliation started. It came home to the congressman of 22 years when he asked his long time close friend, Dr. Arthur Burns, ambassador to the Federal Republic of Germany, for his support in Findley's upcoming election. Burns had privately encouraged Findley saying, "We simply cannot afford to lose you. Your re-election is very important to the entire nation."[12]

But when Findley asked for his public endorsement, Burns replied:

"Oh, I couldn't do that. It's your views on the PLO. I'm sorry."

Findley was publicly called "a practising anti-Semite; one of the worst enemies that Jews and Israel have ever faced in the history of the U.S. Congress."[13] When he tried to speak, Findley was dogged by bomb threats and organized protesters chanting "Paul, Paul, he must go. He supports the PLO." Word was passed around to other Republican candidates on the campaign trail, "Appear friendly with Findley and you lose votes." Ronald Reagan managers issued orders, "Under no circumstances is Findley to get near Reagan." Bob Hope, a personal friend who had previously said, "We need men in Congress who speak their minds" had agreed to help in the 1980 Findley campaign.[14] Yet suddenly Hope backed out of his public engagement on Findley's behalf. Findley, who had promoted and affirmed Hope, couldn't even get a call through or a letter answered. Finally, when Bob Hope did call, he said, "It's too much pressure. I don't want to get involved."[15] President Gerald Ford, a 16-year political colleague, had also agreed to appear on behalf of Findley, but suddenly admitted fabricating a conflict. "Paul, I've got to be candid. My problem is your relationship, your attitude with the PLO and Arafat."[16]

Congressman Findley got the message. No matter how moral the cause, no matter how hopeful the chances for peace, the pro-Zionist lobby will not allow any criticism of Israel or praise of Palestine. The Associated Press reported that "Israel's American supporters again are pouring money into the emotional drive to unseat Central Illinois' Representative Paul Findley."

Findley's district was swamped with Jewish canvassers, including 200 students bussed in by AIPAC to ring doorbells two weeks before the election. AIPAC donated over $100,000 to Findley's opponent; more than half of it had come from out-of-state contributors. Findley lost. AIPAC claimed credit for his defeat.

In his book, *They Dare to Speak Out,* Findley writes:

It is no overstatement to say that AIPAC has effectively gained control of virtually all of Capitol Hill's action on Middle East policy. Almost without exception, House and Senate members do its bidding, because most of them consider AIPAC to be the direct Capitol Hill representative of a political force that can make or break their chances at election time."[17]

He further notes:

In practice, the lobby groups function as an informal extension of the Israeli government. This was illustrated when AIPAC helped draft the official statement defending Israel's 1981 bombing of the Iraqi nuclear reactor, then issued it the same hour as Israel's embassy."[18]

Most congressional actions affecting Middle East policy are either approved or initiated by AIPAC[19] which maintains daily telephone contact with the Israeli embassy.

Another means of influencing Congress is by sponsoring trips to the "holy" land. Over half the membership of Congress has traveled to Israel, about half going on what is deemed official business at the expense of the U.S. government. With few exceptions, Jewish organizations or individuals paid the expenses of the rest.[20] At the same time, AIPAC successfully keeps most lawmakers from visiting Arab countries:

> When the National Association of Arab Americans, working through the World Affairs Council of Amman, invited all Congressmen and their spouses to an expense-paid tour of Jordan with a side trip to the West Bank in 1983, a notice in AIPAC's Near East Report quickly chilled prospects for participation. It questioned how Amman, without Israeli cooperation, could get the tourist across the Jordan River for events scheduled in the West Bank. It also quoted Don Sundquist, a republican Congressman from Tennessee, as expressing "fear" that if any of his colleagues accepted the trip they would be "used" by anti-Israeli propagandist. Only three Congressmen made the trip. A 1984 tour was cancelled for lack of acceptances."[21]

The Story of Pete McCloskey

Most Congress members, fearing lobby pressure, find ways to avoid making statements or taking stands on matters critical of Israel. Not so of Pete McCloskey. He openly criticized Israel and soon found himself voted out of office. In June, 1980, McCloskey offered an amendment calling for the end to the building of Israeli settlements in the West Bank, which the administration itself had labeled illegal. To put pressure on Israel, he wanted the U.S. to cut aid by $150 million, the amount he estimated that Israel was spending on settlement construction. Representative James Johnson declared that many on Capitol Hill opposed Israel's expansion of settlements but:

> Congress was incapable of taking action contrary to Israeli policy. "I would like to point out the real reason that this Congress will not deal with the gentleman's amendment is because [it] concerns the nation of Israel."[22]

AIPAC takes notice of "boat rockers" like Pete McCloskey. He used to be faithful. After a trip to the Middle East in 1979, McCloskey concluded that Israel's policies were not in America's best interest. That started the AIPAC attack.

> An article in the *B'nai B'rith Messenger* charged that: McCloskey had proposed that all rabbis be required to register as foreign agents, declaring that he had made the proposal in a meeting with the editors of the *Los Angeles Times*. The author assured his readers that this tidbit came from a "very reliable source," and the charge was published nationally. The charge was a complete fabrication, and *Times* editor Tony Day was quick to back up McCloskey's denial.

The Messenger published a retraction a month later, but the accusation lingered on.[23] Two years later, AIPAC was still repeating this charge as fact, and described McCloskey as "bitter" with "an intense sense of hostility" toward Jews.[24] McCloskey's opposition to the Lebanon massacres brought reprisals. Sources of Jewish financial support dried up. After losing his next election, McCloskey attempted to return to his old law firm in Palo Alto, which he had helped start. Immediately the firm faced client withdrawals because "a known anti-Semite who supported the PLO and Arafat" was back on staff. The Anti-Defamation League of B'nai B'rith joined in distributing parts of McCloskey's former speeches, with commentary to show his anti-Semitism. When McCloskey accepted an invitation to teach at Stanford, the local Jewish Club called the invitation "a slap in the face of the Jewish community."

McCloskey concludes:

> When I ran for re-election in 1980, I was asked a question about peace in the Middle East, and I said if we were going to have peace in the Middle East we members of Congress

were going to have to stand up to our Jewish constituents and respectfully disagree with them on Israel. Well, the next day the Anti-Defamation League of B'nai B'rith accused me of fermenting anti-Semitism, saying that my remarks were patently anti-Semitic.[25]

McCloskey has not held public office since and he has been promised by the Lobby that he never will again.

Adlai E. Stevenson

Adlai E. Stevenson had an almost unblemished pro-Israel record as a U.S. Senator. In his 1981 bid for re-election as governor, many members of his campaign team were Jewish, including the president emeritus of B'nai B'rith and the director of the Conference of Presidents of Major Jewish Organizations. His Finance and Press secretaries were Jewish. His running mate for Lt. Governor, Grace Mary Stern, was the wife of a man prominent in Jewish affairs. It was said of Adlai Stevenson:

> The make-up of his campaign organization, the character of his campaign, and the support he had received in the past in Jewish neighborhoods provided little hint of trouble ahead from pro-Israeli quarters. Stevenson had received honors from Jewish groups in preceding years. He had been selected by the Chicago Jewish community as 1974 Israel Bond "Man of the Year," commended by the American Jewish Committee for his legislative work against the Arab Boycott on Israel in 1977, and honored by the government of Israel – which established the Adlai E. Stevenson III Chair at the Weizmann Institute of Science at Rehovot.[26]

Yet, in spite of his record, the Jewish Community labeled him "an enemy of Israel and the ally of the PLO," and plotted his defeat. AIPAC in Washington provided a document presenting a summary of Stevenson's Senate actions on Middle East issues; it made no mention of his almost unblemished record of support for Israel and the tributes to him by the Jewish community. Like most AIPAC documents, it would win no prizes for balance and objectivity.

For example, AIPAC pulled from a 21-page report Stevenson prepared after a 1976 trip to the Middle East this lonely phrase, grossly taken out of context: "There is no organization other than the PLO with a broadly recognized claim to represent the Palestinians." This was a simple statement of fact. But the writer of the Jewish Chicago article, citing the AIPAC "summary," asserted that these words had helped to give Stevenson "a reputation as one of the harshest critics of both Israeli policy and of U.S. support for the Jewish state." Stevenson's assessment of the PLO's standing in the Palestinian community was interpreted as an assault on Israel.[27]

What really happened was that in 1980, Stevenson had sponsored an amendment to reduce aid to Israel. He was concerned about Israel's policy of building settlements declared illegal by Presidents Nixon, Ford and Carter. After the vote, Stevenson recalls, he received apologetic comments. "Several Senators came up and said, 'Adlai, you are right, but you understand why I had to vote against you. Maybe next time.'"[28] Chicago rabbis spoke out against Stevenson and thousands of pamphlets attacking him were distributed. Stevenson was actually accused of trying to undermine the very anti-boycott effort that he had in fact sponsored. Campaign funds from Jewish supporters dried up so much so that by election time, his opponent was able to outspend Stevenson by "better than two to one."

Stevenson was defeated amid charges of mysterious irregularities. *Time* magazine describes the election as:

So improbable, so coincidental, so questionable that it could have happened only in Wonderland, or the Windy City. On election night ballot boxes from fifteen Chicago precincts inexplicably disappeared,and others turned up in the homes or cars of poll workers. Stevenson asked for a recount – past records had results in shifts of 5000 to 7000 votes – but the Illinois Supreme Court, by a 4 to 3 vote, denied his petition. Thomas A. Dine, Executive Director of AIPAC, gloated: The memory of Adlai Stevenson's hostility toward Israel during his Senate tenure lost him the Jewish vote in Illinois – and that cost him the gubernatorial election.[29]

Stevenson writes:

There is an intimidating, activist minority of American Jews that supports the decisions of the Israeli government, right or wrong... The Prime Minister of Israel has far more influence

over American foreign policy in the Middle East than over
the policies of his own government generally.[30]

OFFICIAL "LEAKS" TO ISRAEL

Ex-Congressman Paul Findley expresses concern over
leaks from Washington. He records the testimony of a U.S.
ambassador:

"Leaks to Israel are fantastic. If I have something I want
the Secretary of State to know but don't want Israel to know,
I must wait till I have a chance to see him personally."

This declaration comes from an ambassador still on active
duty in a top assignment, reviewing his long career in
numerous posts in the Middle East. Although hardly a
household name in the United States, his is one of America's
best-known abroad. Interviewed in the State Department, he
speaks deliberately, choosing his words, carefully.

"It is a fact that everyone in authority is reluctant to put
anything on paper that concerns Israel if it is to be withheld
from Israel's knowledge," says the veteran. "Nor do such people even feel free to speak in a crowded room of such things."

The diplomat offers an example from his own experience.
"I received a call from a friend of mine in the Jewish community who wanted to warn me, as a friend, that all details of a
lengthy document on Middle East policy that I had just dis-
patched overseas were 'out'." The document was classified
top secret, the diplomat recalls. "I didn't believe what he said,
so my friend read me every word of it over the phone."[31]

Findley, who has spent years researching the relationship
between our government and Israel, goes on to quote an
ambassador still on active duty in a top assignment, saying
"We just don't dare put sensitive items on paper." Findley
expounds:

A factor making the pervasive insecurity even greater is the
knowledge that leaks of secrets to Israel, even when noticed
– which is rare –are never investigated. Whatever intelligence
the Israelis want, whether political or technical, they obtain
promptly and without cost at the source. Officials who
normally would work vigilantly to protect our national interest
by identifying leaks and bringing charges against the
offenders are demoralized. In fact, they are disinclined even
to question Israel's tactics for fear this activity will cause the

Israeli lobby to mark them as trouble-makers and take measures to nullify their efforts, or even harm their careers...[32]

John C. West, ambassador to Saudi Arabia, referring to leaks to Israel recalls:

I would never put anything in any cable that was critical of Israel. Still, because of the grapevine, there was never any secret from the government of Israel. The Israelis knew everything, usually by the time it got to Washington. I can say that without qualification.[33]

PENETRATING THE "IMPENETRABLE" PENTAGON

To protect American security is the Pentagon's first priority. It's inconceivable to think that a foreign nation could penetrate our Defense Department, yet in spite of the most sophisticated security systems in the world, armed guards at every turn, and special advanced clearances, apparently this occurs — and with the knowledge of those charged with our national security.

During the 1973 Yom Kippur War, Israel desperately wanted weapons, especially tanks. Where, but from its own godfather, the U.S.A.? Henry Kissinger's store was always open. Israel was promised tanks from U.S. active duty stock, from reserved units, or straight off the assembly line if necessary. Israel wanted the top of the line, latest model, equipped with the most efficient new guns, but the Pentagon couldn't find them, even by stripping U.S. forces. Earlier models with smaller 90-millimeter guns were sent. Israel objected to "second-hand junk."

Later, according to Thomas Pianka, an officer serving with the International Security Agency of the Pentagon, they searched, but could not find a supply of the needed 90-millimeter rounds. In essence, the Pentagon sent word to Israel:

"Sorry, we don't have any of the ammunition you need. We've combed all depots and warehouses, and simply have none."

A few days later the Israelis came back with a surprise

message: "Yes, you do. There are 15,000 rounds in the Marine Corps supply depot in Hawaii." Pianka recalls, "We looked in Hawaii and, sure enough, there they were. The Israelis had found a U.S. supply of 90-millimeter ammunition we couldn't find ourselves."[34]

Such access to Pentagon secrets by Israel was nothing new. During the Six Day war, according to Richard Helms, Director of the CIA, when one of Israel's arms requests was filled with the wrong items:

> Israeli officials resubmitted the request complete with all the supposedly top-secret numbers and a note to Helms that said the Pentagon perhaps had not understood exactly which items were needed. "It was a way for them to show me that they knew exactly what they wanted," Helms says. Helms believed that during this period, no important secret was kept from Israel.[35]

One official of the Pentagon remembers having received a list of military equipment requested by Israel. He assumed Israel had received White House clearance and began searching for the equipment:

> One office instantly returned the list to me with a note: "One of these items is so highly classified you have no right to know that it even exists"... Somehow the Israelis knew about it and acquired precise specifications, cost and top secret code numbers. This meant they had penetrated our research and development labs, our most sensitive facilities.[36]

One of the most bizarre revelations of Israel's penetrating the Pentagon is told by Admiral Thomas Moorer, Chairman of the Joint Chiefs of Staff. Mordecai Gur, Defense attache at the Israeli embassy, demanded a supply of aircraft equipped with Mavericks, air to surface anti-aircraft missiles. The U.S. had only one squadron so equipped. Moorer recalls telling Gur:

> "I can't let you have those aircraft. We have just one squadron. Besides, we've been testifying before Congress convincing them we need this equipment. If we gave you our only squadron, Congress would raise hell with us."

Gur responded: "You get us the airplanes; I'll take care of Congress."

Moorer adds, "And he did." America's only squadron equipped with Mavricks went to Israel. Moorer continues:

If the American people understood what a grip those people have got on our government, they would rise up in arms. Our citizens don't have any idea what goes on.[37]

When Israel sent a list to the Pentagon store, most U.S. officials assumed it had White House clearance. Sometimes it did. Sometimes it was plain theft. One official says: "Israelis were caught in the Pentagon with unauthorized documents, sometimes scooping up the contents of 'in boxes' on desk tops."... No formal charges of espionage have ever been filed... "Our government never made a public issue of it." He adds, "There is a much higher level of espionage by Israel against our government than has ever been publicly admitted."[38]

CONTROLLING THE CAMPUS

It's no secret: the Israeli lobby is so strong and arrogant with power that without apology, it openly invades the college and university campuses of America. AIPAC trains thousands of students on how to promote pro-Israeli influence on campus. Jonathan Kessler, Coordinator of AIPAC's Political Development Program, claims that in four years, AIPAC "has affiliated over 5,000 students on 350 campuses in all 50 states."[39]

Kessler analyses tapes and notes from talks given on campuses that AIPAC might consider pro-Palestinian or anti-Israeli. He sends arguing points to pro-Israeli activists on campus with suggestions of questions that might create division within the audience, and warns against areas of discussion the speaker could handle well. Kessler works to get students elected to student governing bodies which control invitations to campus speakers. When guest speakers critical of Israel are invited by the school administration, Kessler's students accuse the administration of advocating violence or accuse the speakers of being anti-Semitic or pro-PLO, which AIPAC describes as no more nor less than terrorist.

Kessler advocates that: If you make it "hot enough" for the administrators, future events will be discouraged and even turned down rather than scheduled.

Kessler's students receive training - through role-playing and "propaganda response exercises" - in how to counter anti-Israel arguments. These exercises simulate confrontations at pro- and anti-Israel information tables and public forums.[40]

Pamphlets distributed by AIPAC suggest methods of interrupting speakers on campus. Edward Said, Professor of Comparative Literature of Columbia University, who often speaks out of concern for the Palestinians, describes an engagement at the University of Washington in 1983:

> They stood at the door of the auditorium and distributed a blue leaflet which seemed like a program but was in fact a denunciation of me as a "terrorist." There were quotations from the PLO, and things that I had said were mixed in with things they claimed the PLO had said about murdering Jews. The idea was to intimidate me and to intimidate the audience from attending.[41]

In 1983, a group of Third World student organizations at Harvard invited the director of the PLO Information Office in Washington to speak on the theme of "Palestine: Road to Peace in the Middle East."

> AIPAC student group protestors packed the hall and actively disrupted the meeting. "It was just an absolute madhouse inside," recalls one student who was present. "Abdul-Rahman spoke for probably an hour and a half to virtually constant taunting, jeering, insults, screams, shouts and cursing."

According to the *Harvard Law Record:*

> A representative of the Harvard Arab Students Society "struggled" simply to relate a biographical sketch of the speaker and to provide an introduction to his talk. "It was an extremely intimidating atmosphere," recalls the student. "We barely kept the lid on things. I think the fact that these events occurred is a testimony to our perseverance, not to the lack of intimidation. Because the intimidation is really very overt and very strong."
>
> In both cases the protestors used material provided by the Anti-Defamation League of B'nai B'rith.[42]

AIPAC ATTACKS ACADEMIA

Because of comments unfavorable to Israel, college professors have had departmental funds cut, lost their jobs and been harassed by AIPAC, the Anti-Defamation League of B'nai B'rith, and the American Jewish Committee. Student newspaper editors have been forced to retract statements they knew to be true, and have been threatened with expulsion from school. Criticize Israel on the campus and you may get one of those "If I ever catch you alone" phone calls or be ostracized.

Not only does AIPAC assault students and professors, but also the school that allows criticism of Israel or presenting of Arabs in a favorable light. Colleges that attempt to add a class on Middle East Studies showing an Arab perspective find themselves under attack by pro-Israel groups.

In 1977, Swarthmore and two other small colleges in Pennsylvania sought funds to establish a joint Middle East studies program to "raise the consciousness of students about the Middle East situation." It was to be done in accordance with the highest academic standards and was to include Jewish professors. Monies were to be used to fund books for the library, provide classroom courses and provide scholarships to needy Arab students.

Ira Silverman of the American Jewish Committee saw danger in a plan which included academic freedom for historical research, the examination of current events and open exchange of ideas. The American Jewish Committee went to work to kill the program. Immediately, one of the student newspapers published an article falsely accusing the donor of the funds of being "under indictment by a federal grand jury." Even though the writer refused to reveal where he had gotten his information, the AJC assumed its truth.[43]

The day after the accusing article appeared in the student paper, petitions were circulated in the college dining hall calling on the administration to drop the proposal and were signed by 230 students and faculty. At the same time, the Philadelphia Jewish Federation had a letter on the college president's desk. Philadelphia Newspapers ran headlines such as, "Colleges Hesitate in Scandal." The Jewish Community Relations Council, the American Jewish Committee and the Anti-Defamation League of B'nai B'rith also issued a statement:

> It is altogether appropriate that the schools should seriously
> question the wisdom of accepting any grant from such a
> tainted source...[44]

Finally Congressman James Scheuer, who is Jewish and
a Swarthmore alumnus, called President Friend:

> and requested the telephone numbers of the members of the
> college's Board of Managers, "so he could call them at once
> and get them to put a stop to this outrageous thing." Various
> groups tried to enlist faculty intervention.
>   Harrison Wright, a professor of history at Swarthmore,
> recalled later that there "were memos to the whole faculty
> and to the department chairmen by different groups."[45]

The Jewish lobby won.

> In concluding his memo describing the success of the
> American Jewish Committee's efforts to foil the Middle East
> studies program at the three colleges, Ira Silverman wrote:
> Our participation was not widely known on the campuses
> and not reported in the public press as we wished. This is a
> good case history of how we can be effective in working with
> colleges to limit Arab influence on campuses.[46]

In 1980, the University of Arizona's Near Eastern Center
was accused of "running a pro-Arab propaganda network."
Such an accusation was based on material in the library
which the Tucson Jewish Community Council found offensive.

> They objected to one book's reference to Palestine as "the tra-
> ditional homeland of the Arabs," and another description of
> the Palestinian Liberation Organization as "the only legiti-
> mate representative of the Palestinian people." It faulted a
> map for failing to designate Jerusalem as the capital of Israel
> – even though, of course, not even the United States recog-
> nizes it as such – and cited "the pervasive theme throughout
> most materials that Jews are interlopers in an area that right-
> fully belongs to Arabs."[47]

Another complaint by the TJCC was that maps handed
out during the course did not include Israel. One teacher

responded to the complaint: "Of course the map didn't have Israel on it, because the map was of the Ottoman Empire and Israel was not part of the Ottoman Empire."

For such offences, federal funding for the University had been threatened. Therefore William Dever, Chairman of the Oriental Studies Department, of which the Near Eastern Center was a part, said that he would, "personally remove from the library any materials which the Tucson Jewish Community Council found offensive."48 A librarian who had been enrolled in the Middle East Course commented: "If somebody can get to the district and get them to do this without even asking a question, that's what I find frightening."[49]

ATTACK ON THE PULPIT

We will always have the Jerry Falwells and Pat Robertsons who see Israel as being able to do no wrong, for "God has chosen to establish Israel as a sign of the second coming." Yet, more and more mainline preachers are calling Israel to be accountable for the violations of human rights, especially in its treatment of the Palestinians.

In 1981, Bishop James Armstrong, Bishop of the United Methodist Church, sent a letter to Methodist Ministers in Indiana saying: Israel was seen as God's "chosen people" in a servant sense. Israel was not given license to exploit other people. God plays no favorites.[50]

The Very Reverend Frances B. Sayre, Dean of National Cathedral in Washington saw his job as being a "liaison between church and state." As an activist for political and social justice, he explained his sense of responsibility by saying, "Whoever is appointed Dean of a Cathedral has in his hand a marvelous instrument, and he is a coward if he doesn't use it."[51]

During his 27 years as Dean of one of the most prestigious pulpits in America, Sayre had condemned McCarthyism, worked for the civil rights of blacks, and opposed the Viet Nam War. He also developed a growing concern for Israel's treatment of the Palestinians and felt the responsibility of preaching each week to one of the most influential congregations in America. On Palm Sunday, 1972, Dean Sayre honored his pulpit by delivering one of the most powerful sermons on justice ever heard by America:

Now oppressed become oppressor. Arabs are deported; Arabs are imprisoned without charge; Arabs are deprived of the patrimony of their lands and homes; their relatives may not come to settle in Jerusalem; they have neither voice nor happiness in the city that after all is the capital of their religious devotion too!

Because of his name recognition, Dean Sayre represented an immediate threat to the pro-Zionists who could tolerate no criticism of Israel or concern for the Palestinians. Rabbi Joshua O. Haberman of the Washington Hebrew Congregation told Sayre that his sermon was "so distressing to the Israel government that there had even been a cabinet meeting on the subject - what to do about this minister who had been friendly always to the Jews but who was so misguided."

The Washington Jewish Community Council did not lose much time in deciding what to do. They characterized Dean Sayre's sermon as "an outrageous slander." A letter printed in the *Washington Post* simply called Sayre's sermon "non-factual garbage." Letters continued to appear in the Washington papers attacking Sayre, but none dealt with Sayre's message that Israel's policies persecuted and exploited Palestinians. Sayre himself was condemned over and over, not for being wrong in what he said, but for being forthright in saying it. He was immediately labeled anti-Semitic. Israel and the Washington Jewish community played the game that has been around a long time. If you can't discredit the speech, you discredit the speaker.

Even Christians joined in the criticism, dismissing Sayre's charges as hyperbole because, as they explained, many of them had taken groups to Israel on Holy Land Tours, and had seen nothing of injustice or oppression. Of course, they had seen many holy sites, but had not met nor spoken to a single Palestinian, not even Palestinian Christians.

When friends of Sayre urged him to ease up on his criticism of Israel, he responded: "Of course I realized that it would make a big splash," he said. "But if you put it more mildly, as I had [previously], it made no dent at all. So what are you going to do?"[52]

Sayre's phone began to ring, even in the middle of the night. When he answered, he was verbally attacked, or the caller simply hung up. "Even when I went out, I would be accosted rudely by somebody or other who would condemn me in a loud voice." Such harassment continued for about six months, Sayre said, "even to the point where my life was threatened over the phone; so much so that I had the cathedral guards around the house for a while."

Today, Dean Sayre serves as a chaplain to a local hospital on Martha's Vineyard, but has no regular church responsibilities.

ARMAGEDDON THEOLOGY
AND MODERN ISRAEL

It's called Armageddon Theology. It sounds like this:

> God is kind to America only because America has been kind to the Jew. American Christians must involve themselves politically in such a way as to guarantee that America continues to be a friend to the Jews – that is, the Israelis. I believe if we fail to protect Israel, we will cease to be important to God.[53]

And like this:

> If this nation wants her fields to remain white with grain, her scientific achievements to remain notable and her freedom to remain intact, America must continue to stand with Israel. God has blessed America because America has blessed the Jews, His Chosen People.[54]

These are not the words of AIPAC, the American Jewish Committee or Yitzhak Rabin. The declarations of divine-like devotion linking the destiny of America with the State of Israel express none other than the Armageddon Theology of Old Time Gospel Hour Rev. Jerry Falwell. This belief in an Israel for the benefit of "Jews only" is not limited to Jews only. Falwell speaks for millions of Christian fundamentalists who embrace Zionism with as much enthusiasm as Jews ever did.

Millions of American Christians believe that God has given exclusive rights over "Eretz Israel" to Jews. They say that God is locked into a plan leading toward the second coming of Jesus, and the restoration of Jews to Israel is an essential part of it. Nothing else really matters. Israeli atrocities don't count.

On December 2, 1984, Jerry Falwell, preaching of Armageddon, says:

> In the holocaust at Armageddon, the Antichrist will move into the Middle East and place a statue of himself in the Jewish temple, the holy of holies, and demand that the whole world worship him as God... Millions of devout Jews will again be slaughtered at this time (Zechariah 15:8) but a remnant will escape (Zechariah 13:9) and God will supernaturally hide them for Himself for the last three and a half years of the tribulation, some feel in the rose-red city of Petra (located in Jordan). I don't know how, but God will keep them because the Jews are the Chosen People of God.   Into this area the multiplied millions of men at Armageddon – they will doubtless be approaching 400 million in number – will crowd in for the final holocaust of humanity... As Armageddon draws to a close, with millions lying dead, the Lord Jesus will throw the beast and the false prophet (the Antichrist) 'into the lake of fire that burns with brimstone.' And the Lord Jesus will slay all His other enemies who somehow survived Armageddon.[55]

Falwell portrays a horrifying picture of the end of the world. But he did not seem to be sad or even concerned. In fact he concluded his sermon with a big smile, saying, "Hey, it's great being a Christian! We have a wonderful future ahead."

Jerry Falwell maintains an unflinching loyalty to Israel and for it he is rewarded. In addition to the gift of a luxury jet plane, Menachem Begin in 1980 presented Falwell with a medal named after Vladimar Zeev Jabotinsky. Falwell expressed honor to be associated with a man like Jabotinsky. And why not? They share the same belief systems. Both admire power and advocate ruthless violence in achieving it. Of Jabotinsky, it is written:

> He held that Jews settling in Palestine should not be held accountable to the laws of man. "Anyone who believed in justice," he said, "was stupid. No one should trust his neighbor, but rather go fully armed." And Jews should never compromise with the Palestinian Arabs. He insisted on total, unquestioning devotionto the single ideal of establishing a Jewish state. To secure such a state, he urged armed aggression.[56]

In like manner, Falwell claims that the Bible nowhere rebukes the bearing of arms. Falwell condemns the arms race, not for its escalation, but for being too slow. Like Jabotinsky, Falwell sees the peaceful efforts to settle differences in the Middle East as futile. He admires Israel's military mind-set which maintains a big army, lots of tanks and nuclear weapons.

In 1981, when Begin bombed the reactor at Baghdad, he feared a bad reaction in the United States. For support, he didn't call a Jewish senator or a rabbi, he called Falwell. Begin was worried because we Americans supplied F-16s and bombs to Israel for defensive use and Begin had used them for a preemptive strike. So Begin told Falwell, "Get to work for me." And Falwell promised he would do just that. Before hanging up, Falwell told Begin, "Mr. Prime Minister, I want to congratulate you for a mission that made us proud that we manufactured those F-16s."[57]

A year later, in 1982, when Israel used F-16s to ruthlessly bomb Lebanon, massacring more than 19,000 people, and leaving tens of thousands wounded and homeless, 84 percent of them civilians, Falwell had nothing but praise for the invasion. Then, when the news of the massacre of Sabra and Shatilla surfaced, condemning Israel for its part in the slaughter of almost a thousand Palestinians, mostly women and children, Falwell's grief was not for the victims, but for Israel's reputation. He glossed over the horror of the massacre as a lot of propaganda.

Falwell Is Not Alone

Pat Robertson, T.V. evangelist and 1988 candidate for the White House, excused Israel's atrocities:

We are not to weep as the people of the world weep when there are certain tragedies or breakups of the government or system of the world. We are not to wring our hands and say, "Isn't that awful." That isn't awful at all. This is a token, an evident token of our salvation, of where God is taking us.[58]

Such noted preachers as the Reverend W.A. Criswell, pastor of First Baptist Church of Dallas Texas, believe that we must fight the battle of Armageddon, that Christ can return only to Jerusalem and that Israel today is to be blessed by God because it is the same Israel as the Biblical Zion. Criswell, Rex Humbard, Kenneth Copeland, Oral Roberts, Jerry Falwell and in their day, Jim Bakker and Jimmy Swaggart, preach weekly to millions of Americans that Israel must be restored to fight a great battle with Russia before the Christ can come again.

Fundamentalists see Jesus armed with weapons designed to hurt, injure and destroy people. General Jesus, with his headquarters in Jerusalem, may very well make the first strike against his "enemies." Jesus tells us to forgive our enemies, but fundamentalists predict that Jesus himself will release neutron-like bombs upon his enemies. With excitement, they describe the millions that will be burned alive. They quote Zechariah 14:12, "Their flesh shall rot while they are still on their feet, their eyes shall rot in their sockets, and their tongues shall rot in their mouths." And according to Zechariah 13:8-9, "In the whole land, says the Lord, two-thirds shall be cut off and perish, and one third shall be left alive."

All of God's battle plans center around Israel. Those who take the Bible literally visualize a very bloodthirsty god. No wonder they can be so indifferent to the atrocities committed by Israel against a helpless people. Israeli atrocities pale in comparison with the literalist's view of God's military battle plans. Christian fundamentalists view the events surrounding the creation and expansion of Israel as being no less than the welcomed plan of God.

Because God has called Jews to claim all "Biblical Israel," fundamentalists believe that Christians should support the expansion of Israel by any means. Jewish possession of all Israel enhances the return of Christ, they say, it's all fore-ordained in the Bible.

If there was ever a question among fundamentalists about the intent of God for the restoration of Israel as a condition of Christ's return, that doubt was removed by two Biblical resources: *The Scofield Bible*, and Hal Lindsey's *The Late Great Planet Earth*.

The Scofield Bible

Cyrus Ingerson Scofield published a study Bible in 1909 containing his own brand of theology recorded in an elaborate system of footnotes. The only problem was, most readers could not keep clear in their minds where King James stopped and Scofield started. He was read with almost unquestioned authority. He had a lot to say about prophesy and how God divided people into two groups, one chosen and one lost. Scofield proclaimed that God created the world in 4004 B.C., declared Jews to be God's chosen people and that God blesses those who bless Jews. It's as though God has great earthly plans for Jews but only heavenly plans for Christians.

Most significant was Scofield's teaching that all history is divided into seven well-defined compartments called "dispensations." He believed that history is now unfolding in the last climactic period in which Christ will rule for one thousand years from his headquarters in Jerusalem.

In 1948, Scofield readers and many who call themselves "born again" Christians identified the newly founded state of Israel as one and the same as the Biblical Zion. So God gave all the land described in Genesis 15 to the modern state of Israel. Again, according to the research of Grace Halsell:

> Of the 4,000 evangelical-fundamentalists who annually attend the National Religious Broadcasters Convention, an estimated 3,000 are dispensationalists who believe that only a nuclear holocaust can bring Christ back to earth. This message goes out over 1,400 religious stations in America. Of the 80,000 evangelical pastors who broadcast daily over 400 radio stations, a vast majority are dispensationalist.[59]

The Late Great Planet Earth

The second great influence on the fundamentalist's faith was the best selling religious book of the 1970s, Hal Lindsey's *The Late Great Planet Earth*. Hal Lindsey popularized the fundamentalists' countdown and announced the destruction of the al-Aqsa mosque.

> To be specific about Israel's great significance as a sign of the times, there are three things that were to happen. First, the Jewish nation would be reborn in the land of Palestine. Secondly, the Jews would repossess old Jerusalem and the sacred sites. Thirdly, they would rebuild their ancient temple of worship upon its historic site.[60]

According to Lindsey, the first two conditions have been met, but the rebuilding of the temple is yet to be. The only problem is that a billion Muslims claim this same spot as their third holiest place on earth. From there, they say, the prophet Muhammed took an overnight journey into heaven. Any invasion of this site by "infidels" would cause nothing less than World War Three. None the less, Lindsey declares, "Obstacles or no obstacles, it is certain that the temple will be rebuilt. Prophesy demands it." He says that God requires Jews to destroy the Islamic Dome of the Rock and build on its site a third Jewish Temple. For this reason, Jewish terrorists have stormed the Dome with dynamite. Such terrorists are heroes to many fundamentalists who support them with prayers and generous donations of money. Grace Halsell writes:

> Christian fundamentalists who donate generously to the Jewish terrorists include oil and gas tycoon Terry Reisenhoover, a frequent White House visitor; Mission to America chairman Dr. Hilton Sutton, and Dr. James DeLoach, Pastor of Houston's Second Baptist Church who visited me in my Washington D.C. apartment and boasted that he and others had formed a Jerusalem Temple Foundation specifically to aid those intent on destroying the mosque and building a temple. He said they sent $50,000 for the legal defense of Jewish terrorists who were convicted of plotting to destroy the Dome of the Rock.[61]

The Great Tribulation follows the rebuilding of the temple:

> Large numbers of people will be killed, including many Jews. Lindsey fixes the number of Jews to survive the wars and social upheaval as only 144,000, and these will be converted to Christianity. God is going to reveal himself in a special way to 144,000 physical, literal Jews who are going to believe with a vengeance that Jesus is the Messiah. There are going to be 144,000 Jewish Billy Grahams turned loose on this earth – the earth will never know a period of evangelism like this period.[62]

In foretelling the final battle Lindsey gets specific. When the Bible says locusts, with scorpion's tails, Lindsey sees Cobra helicopters with rear end jets spewing nerve gas. All Arabs plus a Russian confederacy will invade Israel. Read

Lindsey and there is nothing of a God of justice. Nothing of a Jesus who said:

> "The Spirit of the Lord is upon me, because he has anointed me to preach good news to the poor. He has sent me to proclaim release to the captives and recovering the sight of the blind, to set at liberty those who are oppressed, to proclaim the acceptable year of the Lord." (Luke 4:18-19)

Over 18 million copies of his book have been bought by preachers, teenagers and politicians. Millions of voters have read Lindsey's prediction of the "Second Coming War" that must take place in Israel. Lindsey even declares that our generation of leaders must destroy the earth. In fact, the countdown has begun. But is anyone taking him seriously? According to James Mills, former president pro-tem of the California State Senate, none other than Ronald Reagan, who "hated Libya because he saw Libya as one of the prophesied enemies of Israel and therefore an enemy of God." Reagan told Mills:

> In the 38th chapter of Ezekiel, it says that the land of Israel will come under attack by the armies of the ungodly nations, and it says that Libya will be among them. Do you understand the significance of that? Libya has now gone communist, and that's a sign that the day of Armageddon isn't far off.[63]

Throughout this whole scenario, Jews remain God's Chosen people to whom God has given the land of Israel to possess forever, because God favors the Jews and only the Jews. But such a theology of God's exclusive favoritism toward the State of Israel depends entirely upon a *selected, literal, inerrant interpretation of the Bible.*

The Problem with Biblical Inerrancy

Many, even in the mainline churches, claim more for the Bible than we have a right to claim. For years, the fundamentalists have required their adherents to accept the Bible as the Word of God because the church declared it to be the Word of God. When Jerry Falwell, Pat Robertson, or Billy Graham waves his Bible and shouts, "The Word of God says...." he makes an assumption. Ask him how he knows it's the Word of God, and he will inevitably admit that he knows it by intuition. He will say, "I believe" or "I know that my faith would not deceive me." In other words, he grounds objectivity in subjective intuition. He reaches within himself to find his authority. But then, once he has declared his basis of authority, he seldom again acknowledges subjectivity. Rather he shouts, "The Word of God says...." We might trust the Bible, but can we place equal value on all its parts? The Bible very clearly declares that God is love. Anytime I read something in the Bible that contradicts the love of God, I re-read it. Jesus tipped the scales in favor of the love of God over anything else the Bible says about God. When we trust what Jesus says about the love of God, we cannot accept what we hear the fundamentalists say about an exclusive, cruel, "Jews only" God. Such a literal, inerrant interpretation of Scripture leaves me with some disturbing questions.

Translations

Which text of the Bible is inerrant? Are we to accept as our authority the Revised Standard Version, the King James, or the original manuscripts (which we don't have)?

No one on Main Street, Jerusalem could have gone out and bought a Bible in the first century, or the second, or the third. None existed. Before the Bible came into being as a book, its message had been handed down orally for centuries from one generation to the next. Fragments of stories, poems, songs, laws and recollected history were passed down from parent to child for as many as fifty generations before anyone put them into writing. The story changed. If you have ever played the child's game, *Rumor,* you know how impossible it is to whisper a message through even a few people and have it remain unchanged. Context, cultural conditioning, and loss of memory influenced and altered oral tradition. It is unreasonable to think that the national interest of Israel did not influence the "memory" of those traditions. Is it not probable that those who wanted God to favor Israel proclaimed a favoritism and credited it to God?

When the Bible was finally written down, the Hebrew text had no vowels or division into words or sentences. It would look something like, *dfghjklwbrtyswpkkmtyghhxjhkdctgkh*, if we had an original text. Unfortunately, all autographed copies of the Old and New Testaments have been lost. Not a single page of original manuscript exists today as far as we know. At best, we have copies of copies. Does it not also seem probable that Israel's national interest filtered into the recording of Israel's sacred history? At least, we have to admit a few textual discrepancies.

Contradictions in Biblical Text

Through copying, errors, not just a degree or two but errors by the thousands, crept into the text. Add the variances within the original language to the changes in meaning that result from translatings, and we simply do not have an infallible text of Scripture. In spite of the Westminster Confession's declaration that "God by His singular care and providence, kept pure in all ages" the Hebrew and Greek text (I-8), there are errors and contradictions in the Bible.

In the first place, the numbers don't agree. According to II Samuel 8:4, David took from Hadadezer 1700 horsemen and 20,000 footmen, but in I Chronicles 18:4, these figures became 1000 chariots, 7000 horsemen, and 20,000 footmen. Then II Samuel 10:18, the numbers change again to 700 chariots and 40,000 horsemen. I Chronicles 19:18 changes it yet again to 7000 chariots and 40,000 horsemen. One text said Solomon had 40,000 stalls (I Kings 4:26) while II Chronicles 9:25 cuts it ten fold to list only 4000 stalls. Paul said 23,000 died of plague (I Corinthians 10:8) but the Old Testament text he quoted says 24,000 died (Numbers 25:9). Paul obviously quoted from memory. Accuracy did not seem that important to him. It was not the letter of Scripture but the biblical message that mattered to him.

These differences in numbers are important only in that they show a human element in "the Word of God." Also, we find varying texts. In one place, God told David to number the people (II Samuel 24:1), but in I Chronicles 21:1, Satan ordered it. Matthew said Judas hanged himself (27:5). But Luke said Judas fell headlong until his bowels gushed out (Acts 1:18). In the resurrection narratives, Mark said a young man greeted Mary at the tomb. Matthew said it was an angel. Luke altered it to two men, and John said it was two angels.

It seems the first century Hebrew claimed a freedom from accuracy that boggles our computer-age minds. Hebrew writers did not intend to be taken literally. Are we to think that such "freedom from accuracy" applied only to things like numbers, but never allowed a little alteration when recording God-ordained promises that favor one people over all others?

Unworthy Text

What should we do with those texts which seem unworthy of the God proclaimed by the prophets and revealed in Jesus? It is hard to believe that the loving Father of Jesus Christ could massacre the people of Canaan (Deuteronomy 2:34), punish children for the sins of their fathers (Exodus 19:26), hack a helpless man to pieces (I Samuel 15:33), inflict righteous Job with disease (Job 2:7-9), be jealous (Exodus 34:14), change his mind (Exodus 34:14), or curse the human beings that he made a little less than the angels (Malachi 2:2). One feels natural outrage when the Psalmist prays that the children of the enemies of Israel may have their heads dashed against the rocks (Psalms 137:9). Such ideas of God dishonor Him if God is as Jesus said He is. Moses may have stretched out his arms over the mountain to exterminate his enemies, but Jesus stretched out his arms on a cross that his enemies might be forgiven.

Much in the Biblical writer's understanding of God seems unworthy of the Father-God revealed in Jesus Christ. Destroying one people to give their land to some favorites is one of them.

Maybe Paul feared an obsession with the literal interpretation of words when he said, "The written code kills but the spirit gives life." (II Cor. 3:6) As Leslie Weatherhead said: "I must, I feel, judge the Bible by Jesus, not Jesus by the Bible."[64]

The Bible as the Living Word

Here, we come to the crux of the matter concerning the authority of the Bible. Our authority is the Word of God, (Capital W) but the Word of God, according to the Bible itself is not a text, but is *a Living Word!* The printed word gives us only a record of the Living Word. When we worship the text, we get into trouble.

I compare the Bible to corn. Corn cannot exist, grow, or be transported without the husk. In the same way, I think the Living Word which comes to us by God's Spirit cannot survive without the printed word, which gives it stability. But we eat the corn, not the husk. We feed on the Living Word, not on the printed record of it.

Maybe this is what Jesus meant when he talked about the wine contained in the wine skins. The Living Word is like the wine; the Bible, like the wineskins. But Jesus found the skins, such things as the temple and the sabbath, dispensable. It is idolatry to raise the skins to the level of wine, yet I fear when it comes to the Bible, we often hold to the skins and let the wine go.

Few reputable scholars argue anymore that we have an infallible text. Yet Televangelists and Christian Zionists preach unchallenged support for the State of Israel as though we do.

Beyond Literal to Essential Meaning

We must not make the Bible exclusively favor any one people. I read it, always asking the same question. "What do these words mean?" As long as Bible study is limited to learning the words, we can only deal with it objectively: Adam said these two things, Eve said three, and so on. Add them up and we can claim to know the text. But it is when we push beyond the words and ask, "But, what do these words mean?" that we discover insights in the Bible that become the Living Word of God for us. We discover its authority for our lives and its universal Good News for all people.

REACHING THE OVAL OFFICE

Most Americans remember that Harry Truman, against the advice of his own top military and diplomatic advisors, almost singlehandedly assured the survival of the new State of Israel by recognizing it just 11 minutes after David Ben Gurion declared the establishment of statehood. Truman breathed the breath of life into Israel. But few Americans remember why. In 1947, Truman had expressed opposition to a state in Palestine. In reaction, Jewish leaders bought newspaper advertising depicting the Holocaust and calling down shame upon the heads of anyone who opposed a homeland, including the President of the United States. When Truman expressed concern for the Palestinians, he received warnings that he would lose Jewish support for his re-election bid in 1948.

Two-thirds of America's Jews lived in New York, Pennsylvania and Illinois. These three states controlled 110 electoral votes. Suddenly, Truman became a public Zionist. When warned that one-sided support of Israel may touch off a bloodbath in Palestine, Truman responded. "I am sorry gentlemen, but I have to answer to hundreds of thousands who are anxious for the success of Zionism. I do not have hundreds of thousands of Arabs among my constituents."[65] Truman made no effort to resolve the conflict between the Jews and Palestinians, a conflict he had helped create. Recognition of Israel paid off. Truman won 75 percent of the Jewish vote. The Chief Rabbi of Israel told Truman, "God put you in your mother's womb so that you would be the instrument to bring about the rebirth of Israel after 2,000 years."[66]

On the other hand, Dwight Eisenhower resisted the pressure of the Jewish lobby and stood up to Israel. In 1953, when Israel began construction of an illegal diversion of the water of the Jordan River, Eisenhower ordered a cancellation of all U.S. aid. He also threatened to revoke the unique laws that grant tax-exemption for any American making contributions to an Israeli tax-exempt institution.[67] As his Secretary of State, John Foster Dulles, said in 1957:

> We cannot have all our policies made in Jerusalem. He (Dulles) told Henry Luce, owner of *Time, Inc.* and a supporter of Israel's position, "I am aware how almost impossible it is in this country to carry out a foreign policy not approved by the Jews. [But] I am going to try to have one. This does not mean that I am anti-Jewish, but I believe in what George Washington said in his farewell address, that an emotional attachment to another country should not interfere."[68]

Dulles went on to criticize the church in America which claims the Jesus of the oppressed as its Lord, saying:

> It is impossible to hold the line because we get no support from the Protestant elements in the country. All we get is battering from the Jews.[69]

Pro-Israel organizations reacted to the Eisenhower-Dulles threats with renewed determination to increase their influence on the American government.

Senator J. William Fulbright, (D - Arkansas) who had become an advocate of Israel's making peace with its Arab neighbors, conducted a hearing in 1960 on "foreign influence buying on Congress." His principle investigation was a Caribbean state suspected of bribing members of Congress to increase sugar quotas. What he found was massive evidence of "Israel tampering with the machinery of American decision-making." He reports:

> I hadn't realized before the hearing that the Jewish lobby was so powerful. I wasn't conscious of what dangerous territory I was in. I didn't know they were subverting the Congress.[70]

Even Jimmy Carter

Because of his religious convictions, Jimmy Carter came into office with a burning desire for peace in the Middle East. He had taken a trip to Israel and visited the occupied territories before the beginning of his presidency. One of his first moves in office was to call for an international peace conference to negotiate a settlement based upon U.N. Resolution 242. In so doing, he stood up to the Israeli lobby and advocated the return of the captured territories and the establishment of a homeland with secure borders for the Palestinians.

Carter will long be remembered for his bringing together a willing Anwar Sadat and an unwilling Menachem Begin into 13 days of negotiations at Camp David. Sadat signed an agreement which in substance violated his pledge to the Arab states, and ultimately cost him his life. He trusted Carter's pledge to secure for the Palestinians the same peace terms he has secured for Egypt. The settlements on Palestinian lands would be frozen until negotiations for peace were fulfilled. Within days, Begin made a speech reneging on his part of the agreement. Within months, work on settlements resumed. Carter was determined to continue pushing for peace, but the pressure was too much. He yielded to lobby pressure and dropped the proposal.

Especially Ronald Reagan

After meeting with Yitzhak Shamir in 1983, Reagan agreed, in addition to a dramatic increase in aid to Israel, to spend $250 million in U.S. money in Israel to finance the manufacture of a new Israeli warplane. U.S. aircraft firms were dismayed. They had never received such aid.

> During the debate of the bill, Democrat Nick J. Rahall of West Virginia was the only Congressman who objected. He saw the provision as threatening U.S. jobs at a time of high unemployment. Approximately 6,000 jobs would be lost as a direct result of taking the $250 million out of the U.S. economy and allowing Israel to spend it on defense articles and services which can just as easily be purchased here in the United States. Americans are being stripped of their tax dollars to build up foreign industry. They should not have to sacrifice their jobs as well.[71]

George W. Ball, a man with the qualities and knowledge of the Middle East to have been considered for Secretary of State by Jimmy Carter, was outspoken in his concern for Israel. Ball wrote in the *Washington Post* that the Reagan Administration's blind support of Israel was not only inconsistent with U.S. interests but also detrimental to Israel as well. Ball concluded:

> When leading members of the American Jewish community give [Israel's] government uncritical and unqualified approbation and encouragement for whatever it chooses to do, while striving so far as possible to overwhelm any criticism of its actions in Congress and in the public media, they are, in my view, doing neither themselves nor the United States a favor.[72]

Ball criticized Reagan by saying:

> He did not demand, as he should have done under the law, that we would exact the penalties provided unless the Israelis stopped murdering civilians with the weapons we had provided them solely for self-defense. Instead he bought them off by committing our own Marines to maintain order while we persuaded the PLO leaders to leave rather than face martyrdom.[73]

MILITARY ASSAULT: THE *U.S.S. LIBERTY*

No one questions the power of the Jewish lobby to penetrate Congress, the Defense Department or the Oval Office, but few of us are prepared to believe powerful lobby machines could pressure the betrayal of American troops under attack. The 1967 attack on the *U.S.S. Liberty* and the subsequent cover-up was one of the most barbarous acts of aggression ever perpetrated against non-engaged United States military personnel. James M. Ennes, Jr., deck officer on the *Liberty*, reports:

> On June 5, 1967, the Six Day War: Jordan agreed to a cease-fire. With most Arab forces in full retreat, the United States and the United Nations pressured Israel to back off. But even now the Israelis prepared to invade Syria...The invasion was to begin Tuesday morning, the eighth of June. But less than three hours before the scheduled assault and less than two hundred miles away, *U.S.S. Liberty* arrived near El Arish. She slowed to five knots and ambled along the coast in good position to intercept radio messages from throughout the war zone, including much of the traffic from the invasion site.[74]

President Johnson had warned Israel that America would come to Israel's aid only in a case of self-defense, but not for an aggressive attack on its neighbors. Israel's plan to grab more land must at least look innocent

After only hours of very one-sided fighting, the war was almost over. The world wanted peace. Moshe Dayan had a problem. Israel had always gained more on the battlefield than at the conference table. So, how could he maintain that the Six Day War was a defensive action while at the same time ordering the deliberate invasion of the Golan Heights? How could Israel invade Syria without the *Liberty* telling the world?

Perhaps someone speculated that if the *Liberty* were to sink, with no survivors, there would be no one to tell. The threat would be gone and who knows, the Arabs or maybe even the Russians could be blamed. Who would suspect our closest ally? At least this much we know: just hours before invading Syria, Israel "invaded" the *U.S.S. Liberty*. Immediately after knocking out the *Liberty*, Israel invaded Syria. Dayan's plan was well-timed. The only failure was that the

Liberty did not sink. By all speculations, it should have. At 2:00 P.M. Israeli jets hit the *Liberty* with rockets, dropped napalm on the bridge and for 20 minutes strafed its decks with machine gun fire:

> In all, the ship sustained 821 holes in her side and decks. Of these more than 100 were rocket size. As the aircraft departed, three torpedo boats tookover the attack, firing five torpedoes, one of which tore a 40-foot hole in the hull, killing 25 sailors. The ship was in flames, dead in the water, listing precariously, and taking water. The crew was ordered to abandon ship. As life-rafts were lowered into the water, the torpedo boats moved closer and shot them to pieces. One boat concentrated machine-gun fire on rafts still on deck as crew members there tried to extinguish the napalm flames. Petty Officer Charles Rowley declares, "They didn't want anyone to live."75

The *U.S.S. Liberty* was an intelligence gathering ship with no combat capacity other than light machine guns for defense.

At 3:15, the last shot was fired, leaving the vessel a combination morgue and hospital. The ship had no engines, no power, no rudder. Fearing further attack, Captain McGonagal, despite severe leg injuries, stayed on the bridge. An Israeli helicopter, its open bay door showing troops in battle gear and a machine gun mounted in an open doorway, passed close to the deck, then left. Other aircraft came and went during the next hour.

Within fifteen minutes of the first attack and more than an hour before the assault ended, fighter planes from the *U.S.S. Saratoga* were in the air ready for a rescue mission under orders "to destroy or drive off any attackers." The carrier was only 30 minutes away, and, with a squadron of fighter planes on deck ready for a routine operation, it was prepared to respond almost instantly.

But the rescue never occurred. Without approval by Washington, the planes could not take aggressive action, even to rescue a U.S. ship confirmed to be under attack. Admiral Donald Engen, then captain of the *America*, the second U.S. carrier in the vicinity, later explained: "President Johnson had a very strict control. Even though we knew the Liberty was under attack, I couldn't just go and order a rescue." The planes were hardly in the air when the voice of Secretary of Defense Robert S. McNamara was heard over Sixth Fleet radios, "Tell the Sixth Fleet to get those aircraft back immediately." They were to have no part in destroying or driving off attackers...

Ahead for the *Liberty* and its ravaged crew were 15 hours of lonely struggle to keep the wounded alive and the vessel afloat. Not until dawn of the next day would the *Liberty* see a U.S. plane or ship."[76]

Cover-up plans were flying in Washington before rescue planes were flying in the Mediterranean. Before help reached the *Liberty*, Israel issued an apology. Although Israel's explanation was full of false statements, Johnson readily accepted it in spite of the fact that, according to Paul Findley, "The CIA had learned a day before the attack that the Israelis planned to sink the ship."[77]

Admiral Isaac Kidd was given the responsibility of conducting an inquiry. In the meantime. Kidd gave orders to the crew:

Answer no questions. If somehow you are backed into a corner, then you may say that it was an accident and that Israel had apologized. You may say nothing else.[78]

An Associated Press story filed from Malta, the first port reached by the *Liberty*, reported that "senior crewmen" on the ship were convinced the Israelis knew the ship was American before they attacked. "We were flying the Stars and Stripes and it's absolutely impossible that they shouldn't know who we were." Yet the navy disputed their story, saying the U.S. "thoroughly accepted the Israeli apology."[79]

Radio operators on board the *Liberty* heard the Israeli pilots inform their headquarters that it was an American ship.[80] Lieutenant Ennes reports:

Almost immediately the cover-up started. Within a very few hours of the end of the attack and of the word from Washington, we started getting messages from Washington saying, no one will talk about this. All press releases will come from the Pentagon and will be directed by the Pentagon... After the Court of Inquiry you will be free to talk. It took until about June 27th, about another three weeks before the Court of Inquiry's report was produced and released.

It turned out to be what most of us considered an incredible whitewash. It was a report about twenty three pages long.

It made findings of fact and conclusions which were totally opposite of what we had seen. Instead of describing an extended air attack, it indicated that there was maybe five or six minutes of air attack and a single torpedo... The crew was then reminded almost daily in talks given by visitors from Washington that you can't say anything that wasn't in the Court of Inquiry. Any interviews with the press must be cleared with the Public Affairs Officer based in Norfolk. And that's where it stayed.[81]

The *New York Times* said, "It leaves a good many questions unanswered." The *Washington Star*, using the word "cover-up," called the summary an "affront" and demanded a deeper and wider probe.[82]

Israel finally gave to the American Embassy at Tel Aviv an Israeli court of inquiry report known as "Israeli Preliminary Inquiry 1/67" with a request that it not be released to the American people. Carl F. Salans, legal advisor to the secretary of state studied Israel's Preliminary 1/67 item by item and declared that the "Israeli excuse could not be believed."

The items Salans examined were the speed and direction of the *Liberty*, aircraft surveillance, identification by Israeli aircraft, identification of torpedo boats, flag and identification markings, and time sequence of attacks. In each instance, eyewitness testimony or known facts disputed the Israeli claims of innocent error."[83]

Admiral Thomas L. Moorer, retired Chairman, Joint Chief of Staff, still wants an investigation. He scoffs at the mistaken identity theory. Asked why the Johnson administration ordered the cover-up, Moorer is blunt:

The clampdown was not actually for security reasons but for domestic political reasons. I don't think there is any question about it. What other reason could there have been? President Johnson was worried about the reaction of Jewish voters.

Moorer says the attack was "absolutely deliberate" and adds, "The American people would be goddam mad if they knew what goes on."[84] Twenty years later he still charges cover-up:

Well, I think the motive seems to be very apparent, namely
the Israelis were preparing to attack in the Golan Heights
and they did not want the United States Government to know
that this attack was pending...[85]

Obviously, the Israelis had no compunction about
disregarding U.S. wishes. That they were prepared to attack
U.S. military personnel to achieve their designs, however,
and top do it with the willing or the curious complicity of
those in U.S. high office, can only indicate the magnitude of
Israeli influences in America.

Chapter Seven

JUSTICE AND THE PEACE PROCESS

The problem in writing about the Israeli/Palestinian tragedy is that there is no place to put a period. Before the end of the sentence, the situation has changed. Since I began writing this book, the Middle East has experienced the Persian Gulf War, a $10 billion dollar loan guarantee, and the election of Yitzhak Rabin. A new president has been elected in the United States. Even as I write, Jews and Arabs, both in the Middle East and America, are celebrating the new peace agreement between Israel and the PLO. I called a Palestinian friend to ask what he thought about such unexpected happenings, and he wept. "I never thought I would live to see Palestinians treated with respect as we saw in the Washington signings."

"It's a beginning," I said. "The first step toward peace. But I am aware that it is only a beginning and a small one at that. The essential ingredient will continue to be justice."

"Then will it work?" he asked.

"It can," I answered, "But it will be tough."

Palestinians have been taking it on the chin for decades and many Americans have the impression that peace is just around the corner, brought about by one awesome handshake. Even as I write, a television preacher is shouting about the fulfillment of Biblical prophesy that promises peace to Israel. "These are exciting times," he said. "Just think, peace...peace and secure borders for Israel in our time. God has done what all the leaders of Israel and half a century of U.S. presidents have tried to do and failed."

But who can seriously believe that peace can come so easily? It's true, leaders influence perceptions. For years, the Soviet Union was "the evil empire." Suddenly, our president began talking about how things had changed and how we must protect Russia. When perceptions change, enemies become friends. China was portrayed as a backward cruel nation. Then suddenly, China was seen as an economic partner and almost overnight, we have a new trade relationship with China. Leaders can greatly influence the perception of a new Israel and a peaceful Palestinian. But peace will require more than perception. Injustice toward the Palestinians has destroyed the best efforts of the most committed people in the world to bring about peace in the Middle East. Israel and the U.S. share a burden of guilt for the enormous pain felt by the people of that region. Our president speaks of peace and Israel has a new Prime Minister elected on a "Land for Peace" ticket. But peace will not be built upon land. The formula is "Justice for peace."

It is easier for our president to make up with the Soviet Union and China. We don't have a history of economic oppression by the Russians. China has not taken our homes, imprisoned, tortured and deported members of our family. We have no history of suffering at the hands of our "evil enemies." But how will the Palestinians forget if they are not accorded some measure of justice?

REMEMBER THE HISTORY

In the interest of protecting Palestinians against injustice, the Balfour Declaration of 1917 stated:

> It being clearly understood that nothing shall be done which may prejudice the civil and religious rights of existing non-Jewish Communities in Palestine.

No way, so states the rational mind. Conflict between these two nations of people may well have been unavoidable even if Balfour had been serious in his commitment to equally sharing the Palestinian land. But there is little evidence that he or "his Majesty's Government" had any intentions of creating anything but an Israeli-dominant country. The Balfour Declaration starts with commitment to Zionism:

> His Majesty's Government view with favor the establishment in Palestine of a national home for Jewish People, and will use their best endeavors to facilitate the achievement of this object...

How could the Jews be given a homeland on top of the 700,000 Palestinians already living in the land without prejudicing their rights? It seems that Britain never intended to protect the rights of anyone but the Jews. According to Balfour's own words, he had no desire to be fair. In 1919, in a memorandum to the British Cabinet, he wrote:

> In Palestine we do not propose even to go through the form of consulting the wishes of the present inhabitants of the country. So far as Palestine is concerned, [we] have made no statement of fact which is not admittedly wrong, and no declaration of policy which at least in the letter [we] have not always intended to violate."[1]

The Balfour agreement referred to the Jewish community by name. The Arabs, who made up 90 percent of the population, were merely called "non-Jewish sections." In one brief statement, Lord Balfour disenfranchised a whole nation of people and thirteen centuries of history.

The Zionist purpose is not and never has been merely to exploit the Palestinians. Classical imperial movements during the 19th and 20th centuries colonized weaker nations in order to capitalize on cheap labor and extract natural resources. Zionism, on the other hand, wanted to dispossess the Palestinians altogether; its goal was to substitute one people on the land for another. Zionist propaganda insisted that Palestine was an unpopulated wasteland.

When Jews began to move into Palestine at the turn of the century, Jewish capitalists with monies donated from all around the world began to buy up land. At first, the Palestinians welcomed the Jews. In fact, until the Balfour Declaration, Palestinians were extremely tolerant. There was no organized Jew-hating in Palestine and no massacres. But then Zionism began to change things. Zionists refused to recognize Arab rights, or to care what problems a Jewish presence created for Arabs.

Zionist leaders adopted policies of extreme repression of Arab economic, social and cultural life to convince Palestinians it would be best to leave. Jewish immigrants went to Palestine, not to seek a haven within an existing society, but to replace that society. Jewish landowners and industrialists adopted a policy of "hiring Jews and only Jews." Zionist businesses which hired Palestinians were boycotted. Land bought by Jews became inalienable property of the Jewish people. It could never be resold to Arabs, nor could any Arab be employed on it. Jewish migration continued to increase. By 1935, Zionists began more and more to rule the indigenous people. With the help of the British and tax exempt status on imports, Jews soon controlled 872 of a total of 1212 industrial firms in Palestine.

Arabs lacked the ability to defend their land or themselves. Zionist forces, integrated with British intelligence, became the enforcers of British rule. By 1938, 5000 Palestinians were imprisoned, many for long terms. Some 148 were executed by hanging. Over 5,000 homes were demolished.[2]

World War II brought a migration explosion. Political leaders searched for a painless way to make it up to the survivors of the holocaust. Zionism had an answer...a homeland for Jews. They had even picked the place: Palestine. Everyone seemed eager to compensate Jews. What did not enter into the guilt mix was what to do about the Palestinians already living in Palestine. Zionists chose to claim, and the non-Arab world chose to believe, that there were no "non-Jewish populations" in Palestine of any significance.

After 2,778 casualties, including 1,462 Arabs, 1,106 Jews, and 181 British soldiers, Britain gave up and decided to evacuate Palestine. In February, 1947, the British Government referred its Palestinian problem to the U.N.. One year later, the U.N. announced a plan to partition Palestine into two separate states.

Israel accepted the plan. Palestine rejected it, claiming that the Holocaust was not their doing. Why should Arabs be forced to suffer for Hitler's crimes? Why should Palestine have to give up 57 percent of its land, including nearly all the best agricultural and citrus lands, 80 percent of cereal areas, 40 percent of all Arab industry, and all the sea shore to some 560,000 Jews, while only 43 percent would remain for the 1,320,000 Palestinians?

Some Zionists also rejected the plan, but for a different reason. Fred J. Khouri, professor of Political Science at Villanova University, points out:

> Extremist groups like the Irgun proclaimed that "the parti-
> tion of the Homeland was illegal and would never be recog-
> nized... Eretz Israel will be restored to the people of Israel.
> All of it and forever." Irgun also warned that partition would

not mean peace and asked Jews to "take up the offense" not merely to repel any possible Arab attacks, but also to enable the Zionists to seize all of Palestine.[3]

Israel today argues that Palestinian Arabs refused to be satisfied with half the land and therefore have forfeited their right to any of it. Naturally the Palestinians rejected a plan to give half of their state to another nation. It seemed unbelievable that the U.N. would take land which it did not own, from a people with whom it did not consult, and give it to a people they did not trust. Arabs naively believed that the injustice of it would cause world concern. It all seemed so illogical and unfair that Jews, who owned 6 percent of the total land area and comprised less than a third of the population, should be granted a state consisting of over one half of their country.

While prior to 1948, there was no state of Israel, Palestine had been organized as a distinct political unit, with a flag, passport, and currency of its own. Its people were recognized as being Palestinian and they gloried in an attachment to the land. They enjoyed a national state no less than Egypt or India, who at that time, like Palestine, were under British protection. Yet overnight, by decree, their land became Israel, Palestinians became refugees and the State of Palestine disappeared.

I ask myself, how would I feel in a similar situation. Suppose one day a government official came to my home in Atlanta and announced, "The United Nations has decided to give Georgia back to the Indians," he said. "The government has provided for your safety by establishing a refugee camp in Texas. A bus will be leaving today at 3 o'clock. Your house, land and business now belong to the Native Americans." When I start to argue, he holds up his submachine gun and says, "You get on the bus...it's for your own good."

The same official announces that Japan thinks this whole program is a good idea and will donate, in the interest of democracy, huge sums of money to help the Native Americans landscape this backward territory into the rose garden they want it to be.

Any analogy can be push too far and this one has its limitations, not the least of which is that Native Americans have a far more legitimate claim to Georgia than the Zionists have to Palestine. Other than a self-serving interpretation of the Bible, there seems to be little rationale and even less justice in giving 56 percent of Palestine to the Israelis. When I imagine myself in a similar situation, I become outraged at the thought of being dispossessed. I may be forced to yield to such fate, but I would never accept it, even if the rest of the world looks away with indifference. Justice for Palestine raises a question.

Whose Territory Is It?

Yasser Arafat announces that he has worked out a peace agreement with Israel based on "limited autonomy" in the territories for the Palestinians. But the question remains: whose land is it? Today when Rabin speaks of "giving" land for peace, we would do well to remember that his offer of the West Bank and Gaza is of stolen land. It is none of Israel that he proposes to "give'" but Palestinian land illegally occupied since 1967.

The Six Day War

From what the Israelis themselves have admitted, as soon as the Soviets began supplying arms to Egypt, Israel was determined to go to war. A former Israeli Director of Military Intelligence said that Israel "would have invented a pretext for war, if circumstances had not been given to them."[4]

What was later known as Nasser's bluff became Israel's pretext. On May 15, 1967, Nasser asked the U.N. to withdraw its security troops and ordered two divisions of Egyptian troops to cross into the Sinai to take up "defensive positions" along Israel's frontier. Then he reimposed the blockade of Israeli ships through the Straits of Tiran. From the record of his conversations with visiting diplomats, this was as far as Nasser intended to go. He was trapped and hoped the U.N. would step back in and force a settlement by diplomatic means to reopen the canal. In other words, he had hoped the international community would get him off the hook. He mistakenly assumed that Israel wanted a settlement. He had given Israel an excuse — for war.

On June 2, the American State Department informed Israel that it had established with Egypt a basis for negotiations which could lead to the ending of the blockade. Nasser had informed the U.S., and therefore Israel, that he was not serious about the blockade. It was a gesture designed to control the events on his side. In short, the U.N., the U.S. and Israel's political leaders knew that Nasser had no intention of aggression. No less a figure than Yitzhak Rabin, who was chief of Staff, said in February 1968, "I do not believe that Nasser wanted war. The two divisions he sent into Sinai on May 14 would not have been enough to unleash an offensive against Israel. He knew it and we knew it."[5] Mattiyahu Peled, former member of the General Staff confirms:

> To pretend that the Egyptian forces massed on our frontiers were in a position to threaten the existence of Israel consti- tutes an insult not only to the intelligence of anyone capable of analyzing this sort of situation, but above all an insult to the Israeli Army.[6]

Israeli cabinet member Mordecai Bentov revealed in 1972 that:

> Israel's "entire story" about "the danger of extermination" was "invented of whole cloth and exaggerated after the fact to jus- tify the annexation of new Arab territories.[7]

By 1982, Israel admitted that it had started the war. Menachem Begin confessed:

> The Egyptian army concentrations in the Sinai approaches do not prove that Nasser was really about to attack us. We must be honest with ourselves. We decided to attack him.[8]

Egypt was no threat to Israel. But Israel had her excuse. Early Monday morning, June 5, 1967, Israeli jets flying low across the Mediterranean to avoid radar detection, turned south and struck the Egyptian air bases from Suez to Cairo. In less the three hours, the Israelis had broken the back of Egypt's air force. By Wednesday, Israel had taken Jerusalem; then by Thursday, the Egyptians, who had fought a bloody battle in Suez and Gaza, surrendered. Three days later, Israel attacked the Golan Heights in spite of what many believe to be a secret deal to leave Syria unmolested.[9] By the end of the week, Israel's occupation of Arab land was four times the size of Israel before the war. All of the territory that had been allotted to the Palestinian Arab State by the 1947 U.N. Partition Plan was now under Israeli control.

To many Palestinians this was a greater defeat than the Jewish State War of 1948. They no longer had hopes that Israel would ever be defeated and they be allowed to return to their lost homes. The arrogance of power had determined their fate, and they knew it. Even those who try to forget the war are constantly reminded of Israel's arrogance of occupation.

Years of Abuse
Camps
For 400 years, Palestinians lived under the rule of the Ottoman Empire on the land that now makes up Israel, West Bank and Gaza. With World War I, the British offered to change all that. In exchange for Arab support in the war, Palestinians were promised independence. That promise was never kept, and the Palestinians again found themselves as occupied by the British as they ever had been by the Ottomans. They continued to hope that someone with a world sense of justice would help them gain self determination.

The Holocaust of World War II put those hopes on the back burner. Little was said about the Palestinians, even as the 1947 United Nation's Partition displaced 700,000 Arabs in favor of Jews. The most positive United Nations action was to raise funds to help feed the destitute Palestinian refugees at a cost of $27 per person, per year.[10]

For years, Palestinian refugees lived in little huts of mud-and-concrete blocks, corrugated roofs, regimented row after row.[20] They could look across the field and see Jews comfortably living on and cultivating the land that used to be theirs. This went on, not for weeks or months, but for years.

Curfews
 U.S.A. Today says:

Lubana Qabah made the mistake of her life this weekend. Seconds after walking onto her balcony with her 3-year-old son to hang some wash, the Palestinian woman lay gasping

139

on the floor with a bullet through her chest. She died in an ambulance about an hour later leaving a husband, the son who saw her shot, and a 25-day-old baby.[12]

Lubana Qabah committed a crime. She broke the curfew. She was not slipping around in the shadows like some clandestine night stalker, she simply walked out of her house to try for a breath of fresh air. Suddenly, the Israeli Border Police saw her fanning the air to cool her son and dry her clothes. It was against the law, at least, against the rules of the curfew. She was killed for it.

Nearly two million Palestinians of the West Bank and Gaza Strip had been made prisoners in their own homes, not because of anything they had done, but because Saddam Hussein had invaded Kuwait. To violate the curfew meant risking arrest, beatings, long term imprisonment, or heavy fines. It was risky to break the curfew, even for a few moments on the balcony. Only someone like a mother of small children, having listened to them cry for long days on end, a mother who had been locked up in her house day and night with poor ventilation, primitive plumbing, no electricity or running water, no relief by having friends over to play, or contact with other nearby family members, nothing to do but sit in her room and wait, would even think of stepping out on a balcony. Finally, in frustration, Lubana took the gamble. She chose to risk a few minutes in the sun with her children, just to experience the outside world, no matter what it might cost.

The price was high. One breath of fresh air and... bing. Lubana lost. The soldier on the beat, probably Lubana's own age, became her prosecuting attorney, judge and executioner. In less time than it takes to write about it, she was sentenced to death with no right of appeal. Execution was instant.

An around the clock curfew for those like Lubana Kabah made for a desperate life. Food was scarce. No one was tolerated out, not even for medical needs. In selected areas, some residents were permitted a few hours a week to search for food, but stores were mostly empty. Trucks were forbidden to make deliveries. Farmers were prohibited from irrigating their crops or feeding their livestock. Those few who had jobs were barred from going to work. The West Bank and Gaza ground to a halt by military law. Citizens became enemies of the state, and any resistance to the curfew was to be treated as an attack. The territories became military zones, off limits to visitors who wanted to help and journalists who wanted to tell about it. While the world looked the other way, shootings, beatings, and tear gassings went unreported.

Uri Avneri, a member of the Knesset, read a letter of protest to the Parliament, written by Israeli soldiers who detailed the instructions given to them by a superior officer regarding curfew violators:

> Anyone you catch outside his home, first thing, you beat him with a truncheon all over his body, except for his head. Don't have pity on anyone. Don't explain anything. Beat first, then after you have finished, explain why. If you catch a small child, get out the whole family, line them up and beat the father before all his children. Don't consider the beating a right, it is your duty. They do not understand any other way.[13]

Michael S. McManus, in his column on Religion and Ethics, reports on a visit into a Palestinian camp in 1988. He quotes a grandmother, Asia Rizk:

> "I am an old woman, living alone. Soldiers came in here breaking windows. They threw my flour, sugar, salt and rice on the floor, and mixed it up, ruining it. I said, 'For God's sake stop.' So they shot me in the shoulder with a rubber bullet, fired tear gas in my house, and threw my Koran on the floor and stepped on it." Of 25 women I interviewed, 80 percent had been beaten or shot.[14]

Multiply this event by thousands upon thousands and we have some idea of the 45 years of constant humiliation which the Palestinians are now expected to forget in order to make the Peace Accords work.

THE PEACE ACCORD

At probably the biggest event in Washington this year, 3,000 guests witnessed two arch enemies give peace a chance. Mr. Rabin fidgeted and shuffled papers from one pocket to another. He applauded timidly and only in response to the nudge of President Clinton did he reach forward to take the hand of Yasser Arafat. Henry Kissinger fought tears; Jimmy Carter cried. Clinton spoke:

Today we bear witness to an extraordinary act in one of history's defining dramas, a drama that began in a time of our ancestors when the word went forth from a sliver of land between the River Jordan and the Mediterranean Sea.

He spoke as though it was the final touchdown of a great victory. The most amazing speaker was Yitzhak Rabin:

We have come from a people, a home, a family that has not known a single year, not a single month in which mothers have not wept for their sons...We who have fought against you, the Palestinians—we say to you today, in a loud and a clear voice, enough of blood and tears. ENOUGH!

Yasser Arafat seemed equally optimistic as he spoke to the Prime Minister of Israel: "We share your values for freedom, justice, and human rights."

All over town people were saying, "I never thought I would live to see Rabin and Arafat standing together." At the signing of the peace accords, only 15 percent of Americans surveyed said that their sympathies were with Arafat. As my friend Bob said, "No matter what happens, if peace fails, I put the blame on Arafat."

The Other Terrorism

The image of Arafat as a terrorist is one all the lovers of Israeli influence in America have promoted for years. However, the distinction between terrorist or freedom fighter exists largely in the eyes of the beholder. Whether you are called a terrorist or freedom fighter depends upon whose side you are on. Most of those called terrorists consider themselves freedom fighters. Before dismissing Palestinians as terrorists, we must be reminded of Zionists' record, of how they acquired the homes, lands, property and country from those whom they now call terrorists. Sami Hadawi wrote:

The Israelis are the last entitled to condemn acts of terrorism and violence, kidnapping, holding of hostages, and even murder, because they were the first to indulge in such evil practices against innocent people in Palestine. As an established state recognized by the United Nations, they have since 1967 added such refinements as torture of prisoners and detainees, collective punishment, expulsion and deportation, destruction of property and confiscation of Arab land."15

Is it less terrorism when it is State terror? Clifford Wright writes:

> Terror comes from both sides. One side has the advantage of using its air force, and the other its suicide missions.
> Has Israel, and Zionists generally, employed terrorism to further their goals? Terror, as a useful and purposeful policy, was first adopted in the modern Middle East by Zionism. The first airplane hijacking was committed by Israel. On December 12, 1954 a civilian Syrian airliner was hijacked by Israel shortly after take-off. The first car-bomb was an invention of the Zionists, as was the assassination of United Nations personnel.[16]

Zionist terror in the 1930s and '40s has been neglected in the discussion about terrorism in the Middle East. Both former prime ministers, Menachem Begin and Yitzhak Shamir, were terrorist commanders responsible for numerous atrocities, including acts against Jews. The archives of the Haganah contain the names of 40 Jews who were killed by Begin's and Shamir's groups.[17] Shmuel Lahis, the Secretary-General of the Jewish Agency until 1981, was a notorious terrorist who personally murdered several dozen Arab civilians during operations in October, 1948.[18] The Zionist record of terror is long and bloody before the creation of the Israel. In the single month of July 1938 the Irgun killed 76 Palestinians in terrorist attacks.[19] The official history of the Irgun describes in glowing terms the murder of 27 Palestinians who were celebrating the British Mandate government's decision to limit Jewish immigration; it also describes the murder, in another incident, of 52 Palestinians when an Irgun member was arrested by the British.[20]

Two Decades of Offering the Olive Branch

By 1971, Arafat had faced a hard reality. Palestinians would have to regain their homeland, not by military might, but by political means. Ten years of struggle brought about a changing attitude in the PLO. Fatah leaders announced that they "needed time to prepare the grassroots psychologically for recognizing a state whose destruction they have pledged for over a quarter of a century."[21]

In November 1974, the UN General Assembly recognized the PLO as the representative of the Palestinians. Yasser Arafat stood before the U.N. and made a statement on behalf of the Palestinian people. "I have come bearing an olive branch and a freedom fighter's gun," he said. "Do not let the branch fall from my hands." He concluded his speech with an offer to the Jews of co-existence. "We include in our perspective all Jews now living in Palestine who choose to live with us in peace and without discrimination." He went on to say, "I announce here that we do not wish the shedding of one drop of either Arab or Jewish blood."

While the PLO Charter speaks of "liberating Palestine... only through means of armed struggle," this 1974 resolution spoke of "establishing a Palestinian state in areas evacuated by Israel." This clearly indicated PLO hopes for diplomatic and political solutions. It supported peaceful proposals which recognized the existence and sovereignty of Israel. Arafat concluded that half a loaf is better than none, thus compromising for a smaller Palestine.

His goal, in 1974, was a five year plan to convince his Palestinians to work not merely for a political settlement, but to accept the loss for all time of 70 percent of their own land. Five years later, in 1979, Arafat said:

> We have turned our people around. No more this silly talk about driving the Jews into the sea. Today my people are prepared to live with the Jews as neighbors in a mini-state of their own. It is a miracle! How far we have traveled in five years.[22]

The PLO had softened its goal. Instead of "driving all Jews into the sea," they began to work for a "Democratic State in Palestine in which Jews and Arabs would have equal rights." By 1977, the PLO announced its willingness to accept a Palestinian state on any part of Palestine from which the Israelis were willing to withdraw or which will be liberated. But the more Arafat sought to compromise, the more Israel escalated their military actions. The more peaceful Arafat became, the more Israel called him a terrorist.

It was precisely to avoid a diplomatic solution based on land for peace that prompted Israel to invade Lebanon. According to Thomas Freedman:

The consensus view in Israel was that Arafat and his men had concentrated too much firepower in southern Lebanon, shelled northern Israel too many times over the years, and were gaining too much international legitimacy. Never mind the number of Israeli casualties (one death in the twelve months before the invasion); the bogey man Arafat had to be tamed.[23]

Israel's greatest fear was that the world might recognize Arafat as the seeker of peace through diplomacy. The stated justification for the invasion of Lebanon was "in order to ensure that the Galilee will no longer be shelled by Katyusha (Russian) rockets."[24] David Shipler questions this stated motive:

In the four years between the previous Israeli invasion of southern Lebanon in 1978, and the invasion of June 6, 1982, a total of 29 people were killed in northern Israel in all forms of attacks from Lebanon, including shelling and border crossings by terrorist, but that for a year before the 1982 invasion, the border was quiet.(Italics added.)[25]

Noam Chomsky says Shipler's account is only half-true:

While the PLO refrained from cross-border actions for a year prior to the Israeli invasion, the border was far from quiet, since Israeli terror continued, killing many civilians; the border was "quiet" only in the racist terms of US discourse... while twenty-nine people were killed in northern Israel from 1978, *thousands were killed by Israeli bombardments in Lebanon...*"[26] (Italics mine)

He goes on to point out:

The PLO observed the U.S.-arranged cease fire of July1981, despite repeated Israeli efforts to evoke some action that could be used as a pretext for the planned invasion, including bombardment in late April 1982 killing two dozen people."[27]

"Throughout April and May the Israelis brazenly broke the ceasefire on a number of occasions by bombing PLO positions in southern Lebanon. Their objective was quite simply to provoke Arafat into returning the fire, to give Sharon the excuse he needed to go."[28]

Then there was an attempt to assassinate the Israeli ambassador in London. Evidence points to Iraqi students of Abu Nidal, a sworn enemy of the PLO, who did not even have an office in Lebanon. Abu Nidal's students gave Sharon the "unquestionable breach" he wanted. In response to an attack on one Israeli citizen in London, Sharon invaded Lebanon. Israel's massacre machine turned Lebanon into a killing field.

The PLO's 15,000 men and boys, including the Lebanese, were ill prepared for war. They had no air force, no navy and very little army. Israel's barbaric onslaught embarrassed not only Israel; even Americans who had supported the policy of "Israel, right or wrong," had to swallow hard. For the first time, the American public began to get a glimpse of Israel's state terrorism.

The reason for the Lebanon invasion had little to do with any PLO threat to the northern Galilee. The real reason for such large scale slaughter was explained by Israel's leading specialist on the Palestinians. Hebrew University Professor Yehoshua Porath, shortly after the invasion was launched, said the decision to invade:

> flowed from the very fact that the cease fire had been observed. This was a "veritable catastrophe" for the Israeli settlement, because it threatened the policy of evading a political settlement. "The government hope," he continued, "is that the stricken PLO, lacking a logistic and territorial base, will return to its earlier terrorism; it will carry out bombings throughout the world, hijack airplanes, and murder m a n y Israelis," and thus will lose part of the political legitimacy it had gained and undercut the danger of negotiations with the representative Palestinian, which would threaten the policy—shared by both major political groupings—of keeping effective control over the occupied territories.[29]

Rabin Talks Peace, But...

We first heard of Yitzhak Rabin as a member of an underground military unit called Palmach which forced thousands of Palestinians from their homes. He broke onto the scene of Israel's history in 1948 when he forced 50,000 to 60,000 Palestinians from the towns of Lydda and Ramlah to flee from their homes. He became chief of staff and launched the Six the Six Day War of 1967, which created hundreds of thousands of Palestinian refugees and captured for Israel the West Bank, Gaza, the Golan Heights, East Jerusalem and the Sinai Peninsula. He also approved the invasion of Lebanon. According to Thomas Freedman:

> None other than Yitzhak Rabin stood with Ariel Sharon on the outskirts of West Beirut in the first month of the war and urged him to 'tighten' his siege of the city and to cut off the water supply.31

As Israel's Defense Minister, he shaped Israel's brutal suppression of the *Intifada*, which:
— approved round the clock curfews
— used food as a weapon
— established the "broken bones" policy
— increased the number of "expulsions" of Palestinians
— suspended judicial procedures for "administrative detentions"
— closed Palestinian schools
— barred reporters from occupied territories
— increased the destruction or sealing of houses

On January 21, 1988, he instructed his troops that "The first priority is to use force, might, beatings." Then he added, "No demonstrators have died from being thwacked on the head."[31] Robert I. Friedman, winner of the Smolar Award for Excellence in North American Jewish Journalism presented by the Council of Jewish Federations, declares such a statement is contradictory to history and fact:

> Children have been the main combatants and the chief victims of the *Intifada*. At least ninety-six of Gaza's children have been killed and more than 23,120 wounded since the beginning of the uprising. Amnon Rubinstein, leader of the liberal Shinui party, called on then-Defence Minister Yitzhak Rabin to investigate the torture of a nine-year-old boy from Gaza's Shati camp, who was said to have been stripped, hung upside down by his feet, and beaten for three hours by Israeli soldiers as an example to young stone throwers. The United Nations Relief and Works Agency (UNRWA) which provides basic services in the refugee camps such as housing, health care and education, filed a complaint with the Israeli military, but has received no reply. Every refugee family I met in

the occupied territories had at least one son in prison, in the hospital, or dead.[32]

While in 1992, as Israel's new Prime Minister, Rabin said, "I am willing to travel today, tomorrow, to Amman, Damascus, Beirut on behalf of peace, because there is no greater triumph than the triumph of peace," both his actions and his words belie that comment:

> Over the years Rabin has repeatedly made clear that he does not favor returning all or even most of the occupied territories. He opposes Palestinian statehood. In his inaugural address, he explicitly ruled out any discussion, much less compromise, of the status of Jerusalem. He implicitly laid claim to major parts of the occupied West Bank, the Golan Heights,and, presumably, the Gaza Strip by stating that he would continue establishing "security" settlements. He made no mention at all of U.N. Resolution 242, which established the formula of trading land for peace, or of the Palestinian Liberation Organization, the Palestinians' sole legitimate representative. He opposes Israeli citizenship for Palestinians in the occupied territories. All this amounts to a hard-line position.[33]

A U.N. Investigative Committee, which Israel barred from visiting the West Bank and Gaza Strip, reported on May 11, 1993 that "More Palestinians were killed, wounded and tortured under Rabin's Labor Coalition than under Shamir."[34] B'Tselem and the Palestinians Human Rights Information Center report that:

> Between January 14th and May 17th, 1993, 34 Palestinian children, aged under 16 have been killed. Among them were a baby of 18 months, a two year old, a five year old, and three ten years old children. Deaths in Gaza Strip alone average one a day since Rabin has become Prime Minister. Palestinian fathers cannot protect their children from being tortured. To underscore their pain, soldiers often beat fathers in front of their children. Fifty-five percent of Gaza children have witnessed such humiliation.[35]

Late in March, 1993, Rabin announced the closing of the borders of the Occupied Territories as a step toward peace. It will serve as an experiment toward independence, he said.

In reality, it is another way of trying to break the backs of Palestinians. Israel has very carefully controlled the Palestinian economy to force the Occupied Territories into total dependence upon Israel. The sealing of the territories barred 120,000 Palestinians from work in Israel, cutting off more than a million people from their only source of livelihood. According to U.N. figures, sealing the territories cost the Gaza Strip $750,000 each day and the West Bank some $2 million per day. Rabin declared that the closure was not temporary. "We must see to it that Palestinians do not swarm among us."[36] In actuality, Rabin has succeeded in erecting a high security fence around the entire Gaza Strip, trapping its 900,000 residents in what may be the world's largest prison.

It appears that the Israelis may be implementing a plan, first proposed in October 1990 by Economics Minister David Magen, to reduce the number of the Palestinian work force in Israel so as to make room for the new Soviet immigrants.[37] A huge influx of Soviet Jews, 200,000 in 1990 and more than 800,000 by the mid-1990s (proportionately like moving the population of France into the U.S.) crowded in on top of a 10 percent unemployment rate. The only jobs Israel has to give are Palestinian jobs. Even though Soviet professionals, doctors, engineers, violinists don't by nature choose to become street sweepers, they take any job they can get, even "Palestinian" work.

A TRY FOR PEACE

It's called a window of opportunity. Rabin and Arafat had only a limited time to open up dialogue and they both knew it. Arafat was nearly bankrupt. He had lost the support of his superpower patron, the Soviet Union. PLO members began to drift away. As Arafat faded, the fundamentalists gained strength. If a compromise could not be reached soon, Arafat and Rabin both knew that they could be overtaken by extremists on both sides—Israeli hardliners and Muslim fundamentalists. Hamas, emerging as an alternative to the PLO, contends that:

> Palestine cannot be given up in part or ceded. No one has this right. No Arab country, nor all the Arab countries together, no king or president, nor all the kings and presidents together

have that right. Neither the PLO nor any other organization has that right because Palestine is entrusted to Muslims for all generations.[38]

Many Palestinians believe that Palestine, all of it, is rightfully theirs. Many Jews, such as far right author Moshe Shamir, say that the agreement is cause for lament. "There has never been a moment during our thousands of years of history when a central national authority has recognized that this land belongs to another people," they say [39]

Yasser Arafat was facing the most pro-Israel president in recent memory. On the other hand, Yitzhak Rabin faces a choice between losing the Jewish majority in Israel by incorporating the Palestinians of the occupied territories into her political system, or seeing Israel become a non-democratic apartheid Jewish state. A major influx of Soviet Jews may delay the inevitable but will not remove it. Count the guns, and Israel dominates today. Count the people and the Palestinians dominate tomorrow, and all Israel knows it. For this reason, 40 percent of Israelis, up from 25 percent two years ago, say they are ready to accept a Palestinian State. Even though many fear that the PLO will not be able to control anti-Israeli terrorism by rival Palestinian groups, *still 51 percent say they trust the PLO.* At least 30 of the 44 Labor Members of the Knesset favored such negotiations.

For Israel, the Gaza Strip is expensive, has no holy places, not much land for settlements, and no historical roots, nothing but troubles. Israeli soldiers resent serving there. The new Israeli is after a good life, relaxation, country clubs and travel abroad, not the responsibility of holding in check a crowded unhealthy concentration camp. If Israel continues its occupation, it will have little financial strength left for such needs as education, health care, housing, industrial development and infrastructure building for the people of Israel.

The present agreement gives only "limited autonomy" over 1.7 percent of historic Palestine, 80 square miles in Gaza and eight miles in Jericho. It is called a beginning. As it stands, Rabin has won a victory that will not only ensure Israel's security and lessen the cost of occupation, but will end the 100-year war with Palestinians on terms that leave Israel in ultimate control of the territories.

So while Arafat and Rabin may be talking to one another, they are leaving some big issues out of their conversation.

STILL HIDDEN IN THE CLOSET

The biggest question is statehood.

1 - STATEHOOD

Palestinians have come a long way from the plan of "throwing the Jews into the sea." Palestinian leaders accept the fact that Israel with three million Jews is here to stay. They have even given up on the goal of building a new society in co-operation with the Jews — one democratic Palestinian state in which Jews and Arabs live in equal citizenship. For more than a decade now the goal has been a "two states solution," with Israel and Palestine living side by side in harmony and economic partnership with one another. Such a compromise is not new. Back in 1971, Abu Iyad envisioned a mini-Palestine:

> We realized that we'd have to devise a political strategy for setting up a state on any part of liberated Palestine soil.[39]

A year later, Said Hammami, the PLO's spokesman in London called for:

> the establishment of a Palestinian state in the West B a n k and Gaza as a means of "drawing out the poison at the heart of Arab-Israeli enmity" and urges Israeli Jews and Palestinian Arabs to "recognize one another as peoples."[40]

The Palestinian National Council in 1973 adopted the idea of "establishing a National Authority on any part of Palestine to be liberated." Before an audience of Arab leaders in Algiers in 1988, Arafat distributed a PLO article announcing its readiness to accept a mini-Palestine in the hopes of peace.

> We believe that all people — the Jewish and the Palestinian included — have the right to run their own affairs, expecting from their neighbors not only non-belligerence but the kind of political and economic co-operation without which no state can be truly secure. The Palestinians want that kind of lasting peace and security for themselves and the Israelis because no one can build his own future on the ruins of another.[41]

Five months later, December 14, 1988, Arafat's message to the United Nations in Geneva called for an international peace conference on the basis of UN Security Council Resolution 242, the pursuit of a "comprehensive settlement," including Israel. That same night, in a press conference before 800 reporters, he repeated:

> We have made our position crystal clear, and accepted "the right of all parties in the Middle East conflict to exist in peace and security, including the State of Palestine, Israel and other neighbors." He added, "I repeat for the record that we totally and absolutely renounce all forms of terrorism."[42]

Although it had taken them a long time, most Palestinians finally accepted what to many seemed to be the unacceptable—a Jewish State on part of "their" Palestine. Church leaders in Israel called for a two-state solution built upon the foundation of justice.

Na'im Ateek, Canon of Saint George's Cathedral in Jerusalem, called for the recognition of the need, though not the right, of the State of Israel to exist. "The elimination of Israel would mean greater injustice to millions of innocent people who know no home except Israel."[43] Ateek carries within his heart a Godly hope, that Jews and Palestinians should share the land. "We are a people not fighting to destroy its neighbors, but a people fighting for the right to be a neighbor."

Statehood is and always has been at the heart of the Palestinian peace struggle. Yet, the biggest unaddressed question of the peace agreement is that of statehood. Arafat is confident that the Accords sew the seed for a Palestinian State. Rabin is equally adamant that statehood is out of the question. The Peace Accords say nothing about Statehood.

2 - SETTLEMENTS

Palestinians were driven from their homes in 1948, again in 1967, and they are still being displaced by settlers. In Gaza, Israel has put 3,000 settlers on chunks of land larger than that on which 600,000 Arabs live. Settlements not only mean the confiscation of land; they create an independent infrastructure of roads, electricity, water, telecommunications and control over public water resources. Even as Rabin gestures about "good will," land is still being confiscated and settlements are still being built at record speed. According to an August 1993 report issued by the Jerusalem Media and Communications Center, land was being taken for roads and "for purposes unknown," despite documents proving Palestinian ownership. Settlers were actively defying the government freeze on expansion of "political" settlements: foundations were being laid for new housing units near Hebron, Ramallah and Nablus. Settlers are still given preferential loans and grants. Pierre Schori, a Swedish Parliamentary delegate who toured the Gaza Strip, describes:

> The situation there is horrifying. It's more like a war zone. I was shocked by the mountains of settlements. Hundreds of thousands of homes create new facts, a new geography.[44]

Some Israelis moved into the territories out of a strong sense of mission, that they are fulfilling a religious obligation. Some claim that the coming of the Messiah depends upon their occupying the lands of "Judah and Samaria." They see the Peace Accords as incompatible with their religious responsibilities. Others ask basic questions about the status of Jews in a land governed by Palestinian laws. According to the Peace Agreement, the more than 300,000 settlers will remain during the interim period and they will be "immune" from Palestinian authority.

On the other hand, Palestinians complain that:

> For the first time the PLO has formally acknowledged the privileged position of the more than 150 Israeli settlements and 300,000 Israeli residents living in the occupied territories. The agreement to permit Israel to maintain complete control over the territories for the foreseeable future illustrates the Palestinians' inability to shape their own future. Israel retains the authority to continue expanding the settlements. The current Israeli population in the Gaza Strip is 4500, in the West Bank 120,000, and in East Jerusalem 160,000.[45]

3 - REFUGEES

What about the 350,000 Palestinians suffering in the 28 refugee camps in the West Bank and Gaza, and those in the 10 camps in Jordan (210,000), 10 camps in Syria (75,000), and 13 camps in Lebanon (150,000)? They all yearn to go home. And what about the 2 to 3 million not living in camps, displaced in the wars of 1948 and 1967, who have still been prevented from returning to their homeland? Has the PLO abandoned their right to return to their homes which are now a part of Israel? The Declaration says that a "Continuing Committee" of representatives from Israel, Egypt, and Jordan will decide with the Palestinians who of the 1967 war refugees may be allowed to return. The *Guardian Weekly*, September 26, quotes a PLO official as saying that 400,000 refugees would be permitted to return during the interim period. Israel has not agreed to this figure, and what about the rest? With natural population growth, the new autonomous area might have to be prepared to absorb around 3.5 million new inhabitants. In a land already densely populated, can the new "limited autonomous" government stay afloat? Will a new "nation" sinking deeper into squalor not become a breeding ground for political unrest and uncontrolled violence? Then will Israel not claim the "obligation" to re-enter the territories and permanently dominate the very subjects she now claims to want to set free? The Peace Agreement has chosen to keep this problem in the closet for now. It will not be easy.

4 - LAND

The Accords' Declaration of Principles states that Israel will cede authority to Palestinians in the areas of education and culture, health, social welfare, direct taxation, and tourism. Yet:

> Prior to the *intifada*, before the large scale resignation of Palestinian employees from the civil administration and an overall breakdown of services, Palestinians had much authority over the very sectors they are now being promised with the exception of taxation. These "new" powers represent little more than what Palestinians had long possessed.[46]

Gaza is a society without leaders. During the uprising, Israeli authorities destroyed Gaza's leadership structure through imprisonment, deportation, and killing. Some ask whether Gaza is governable. How long might it be before Israel moves in, declares martial law and says to the world,

"You see. We gave them a chance. They just can't do it." Without pressure for justice from Bill Clinton, some wonder if Israel is really trading land for peace, or simply trading limited autonomy for time.

5 - WATER

About 40 percent of all water consumed in Israel is tied to the territory taken in 1967. Israel drains more than 600 million cubic meters a year...from the upper Jordan River, the Sea of Galilee, Golan Heights and southern Lebanon. According to Thomas Stauffer:

> Israeli economists estimate that it would cost $1 billion or more each year to replace with desalinated water those diverted water supplies if peace meant Israel had to replenish that water to residents upstream in Lebanon, Syria, Jordan and the West Bank.[47]

THE BOTTOM LINE IS ECONOMICS

The Peace Accords follow years of devastating economic policies forced upon the Occupied Territories by Israel. Frank Collins, who divides his time between Washington and Jerusalem writing for the *Jerusalem Journal*, explains:

> For 24 years of their occupation of the West Bank and Gaza Strip, the Israelis have systematically done everything in their power to block the normal development of the Palestinians' economy. Far from allowing the growth and modernization of the economic infrastructure, the occupation authorities have gone to great lengths to thwart any progress in this direction. They have striven to make the Palestinian economy totally dependent on, and subordinated to, that of Israel... The licensing of a new Palestinian factory requires securing certification from potential Israeli competitors that they will not suffer from the new Palestinian competition. Naturally, very few licenses for new factories are granted. Water consumption by Palestinians is restricted to 1967 levels, with the result that irrigated agriculture has declined from 18 to 5 percent of the Palestinian economy.[48]

Before the Gulf War, every night tens of thousands of laborers left their homes to eke out a living in Israel where they were discriminated against in wages, barred from Israeli unions, and had huge sums deducted from their paychecks. While the income from wages earned in Israel provided an improved standard of living, telephones, tractors, cars, electrical appliances and health care, still it all depended upon Israeli employment.

Over the years of occupation, the West Bank and Gaza had become almost totally dependent upon Israel for trade and employment. The territories received 90% of their imports from Israel and in turn provided laborers to do the unskilled, "dirty" jobs in Israel. These poorly paid workers were not covered by trade unions, nor were they eligible for the most basic social welfare and health benefits.

Palestinians regularly complained of being subjected to abuse, cheated out of their wages, made to work under inhumane conditions, and subjected to body searches accompanied by shouts and shoves, especially at the checkpoints. Cars lined up bumper to bumper for security checks. Many Palestinians were required to stand up against a wall and be frisked. Some complained that their money was taken without cause; identification cards were arbitrarily confiscated. For no reason other than the entertainment of the soldier, Palestinians were made to undergo humiliations such as being forced to bark like a dog or bleat like a sheep. Each day the checkpoint was an ordeal for the Gaza worker who was exposed to the whim of any Israeli in a uniform.

The DataBase project on Palestinian Human Rights reports:

> By 1987, there were an estimated 10,000 unemployed Palestinian college graduates. Many college graduates, including physicians and engineers, worked as day-laborers inside Israel. To create further economic difficulties for the Palestinians, the Israelis have steered visitors away from the Arab businesses in Jerusalem. This strategy, plus the steady decline in tourism have worsened economic conditions.[49]

Israel's goal continued to be to make daily life for the Palestinians so unbearable that the entire population would gradually leave their lands and homes, to be replaced by Jews. Palestinians were already aware of the tremendous gap between living standards of Palestinians in the captured territories and that of the Israeli oppressors they served.

Palestinians have three or more to a room, Israelis one. So, Rabin shakes hands with Arafat. But many look on and wonder.

WHY NOT A $10 BILLION LOAN GUARANTEE FOR PALESTINE AND PEACE?

For the Peace Accords to work, Palestinians will need sizable aid and financial investments. At the time of this writing, international donors have pledged almost $2 billion to help rebuild Palestine. The World Bank estimates that $5.5 billion would be needed over 10 years to improve basic services in the Occupied Territories, including industrial parks, waterworks, sewage systems, houses, hospitals and schools.[50]

Yet, most Americans, 54 percent of those surveyed, oppose assisting Palestinians with U.S. economic aid. Most said that their sympathy was with the PLO and not with Israel. Yet sixty percent said that they do not trust the PLO.

"You've got to be kidding," my friend Bob said. "How on earth do you ever expect the Palestinians to repay?"

"That was never a concern when we doled out billions for Israel," I said. "Now it's needed for peace."

Because of its poor credit ratings, no one would loan Israel money without a United States guarantee of repayment. For more than a year, Bush had insisted that such monies not be used for construction of illegal housing in the captured territories. Yet within a month of election day, Bush dropped any linkage. In spite of the fact that 80 percent of Americans oppose co-signing the loan, Congress approved the guarantees on October 1, 1992 *without a debate.* In addition to the amount set aside required by law, which could be up to $800 million, the American taxpayer will be required to cover all defaults including interest.

Israel cannot repay. Since 1985, Israel has not paid back one penny of its aid loans. All loans have been redefined as grants by the U.S. Congress. The Cranston Amendment guarantees that U.S. grants to Israel will continue to match that which Israel owes back to the U.S.. The combined direct and indirect cost to the U.S. economy for support of Israel totals $163 billion, according to George and Douglas Ball. Those less conservative would add another $100 billion to that total. That's approximately $1,000 for every American living today.

From 1949 until the end of 1991, the U.S. taxpayer has provided Israel with $107 billion in aid and special interest, in spite of the fact that U.S. law (502-B) provides for the termination of aid to any nation that develops nuclear weapons or engages in a consistent pattern of "gross violations of internationally recognized human rights."

When it looked like President Bush might defy the Jewish lobby and hold up the loan guarantee, major Jewish organizations in America trying to gain guarantees from private citizens, approached:

> twenty Jewish billionaires in the U.S., selected from a list of the 500 richest persons in the world, asking them to guarantee Israel's loans of Soviet immigration absorption. All twenty, who support Israel politically, flatly refused. They claimed that as businessmen motivated solely by considerations of profitability, they could not guarantee loans to a state considered such a risky case in respect to its repayment ability.[51]

Who can blame them? The U.S. government's Export-Import Bank has given Israel a rating of D on a scale of A to F. Standard and Poor's gave a B-minus, which is the lowest investment grade on its index. According to Dr. Israel Shahak, Holocaust survivor and professor at the Hebrew University in Jerusalem:

> In order to repay this sum each year, Israel would have to increase its exports by at least $4 billion, or more if profits from such exports did not reach 50 percent. However, the last officially recorded value for Israeli exports was some $9.4 billion in 1988. The value of imports was $12.3 billion, yielding a trade deficit of 23.2 percent. Zvi Timor, Israeli economist writes, *"An increase of Israeli exports by $4 billion, or some 43 percent in a single year is absolutely impossible."*[52]

Someone said that is you liked the S&L bailout, you are going to love the $10 billion Israeli loan guarantee.

President Clinton fired U.S. Ambassador William Harrop for warning that Israel may be facing a cut in foreign aid, saying that Harrop "deviated" from U.S. policy.

Four billion a year, which is the published figure, is serious enough, considering the American deficit. But according to *The Washington Report for Middle East Affairs,* the real cost, hidden in the budget including grants, interest, loan guarantees and compounded interest on previous grants comes to the staggering sum of $11,321 billion for FY 1993. That amounts to $17,317,808 per day, 365 days a year. On April 1, 1993, the Clinton administration announced a plan to immunize every American child against nine diseases at a cost of $1 billion, but there is no money. This care to America's population of 260 million people could be funded by 57.7 days of US taxpayers money sent to support the 5 million people of Israel. But the big losers are the Palestinians who now, more than ever, have their occupation paid for by the U.S..

In spite of Israel's claim to want money for humanitarian reasons—the resettlement of Soviet Jews— *The Washington Jewish Week* announced:

> The loan guarantees will serve purposes in Israel that are strikingly nonhumanitarian, investing in infrastructure, bolstering foreign currency reserves,and making cheap loans to the business community.[53]

It will be money used directly or indirectly to build settlements in the captured territories, which the US has declared illegal. Michael Lerner, editor of *Tikkun* wrote:

> This is the fault of Shamir, not Bush...Shamir is trying to create facts on the West Bank that would make a land for peace exchange impossible. Now he is demanding that the US give him money to subvert American policy. What kind of chutzah is that?"[54]

Once again the U.S. joins in Israel's theft of Palestinain lands by financing "facts on the ground" to make land for peace impossible without an all-out war. If U.S. taxpayers are to be asked to support a $10 billion expenditure in the Middle East, why not spend it on Palestinian development and peace?

Nearly two thirds of Palestinians back the accords, not because they think it is right, but because they hope it is a step in the right direction. The essential ingredient is justice. The last thing those who have been oppressed by occupation for 24 years will tolerate is more oppression, even in the name of peace.

If we want peace, we must work for justice.

Chapter Eight

WHAT CHRISTIANS CAN DO

Over and over again, those who hear me speaking on behalf of the Palestinians ask, "But, what can we do?" In this chapter, I will attempt to put some handles on what an ordinary Christian in an ordinary church in America can do for the Palestinians in the interest of justice. The options seem quite limited, but we must find a way—for their sake and ours.

I. WE CAN FIND WAYS TO LEARN

We cannot allow others to dictate our thinking on any subject, especially on anything as important as Christian faithfulness, which is tested by an attitude towards seeking justice for the oppressed. It's a Christian's duty to know.

To begin learning, we must overcome our reluctance to hear about unpleasant things or to reverse our preconceived notions. More often than I would like, people say to me, "We come to church to be comforted, Tom, not to be disturbed."

I understand. By nature, we would prefer to laugh, to hear pleasant stories and believe all is right with the world. To hear of such horrendous violations of human rights as those which are taking place in Israel today, to read in detail of the kinds of torture recorded here, and to have to admit to government cover-ups by those we have always revered, shatters any hope of comfort and "church as usual." Yet, in view of all the evidence surfacing around us, we cannot ignore what is going on in the contemporary, secular state of Israel.

We Can Read

Anyone who takes seriously all that has been said in this book must by now be asking, "Where does this writer get all this?" My enlightenment began with the reading of Na'im Ateek's book, *Justice and Only Justice*. I list here those resources that have helped me. High on my list and the best books to read first are:

1 - *Justice and Only Justice*, Na'im Ateek
This short 188-page book by a Palestinian Christian offers a first hand accounting of the injustice felt by the victims of the state of Israel. Na'im Ateek, whom I have come to know and love, promotes reconciliation of Jews and Palestinians on the Biblical admonition to "Do justice, and to love kindness, and to walk humbly with your God." (Micah 6:18) Ateek calls upon a Biblical understanding of God as our hope for peace. This is an excellent book for anyone beginning to examine the Christian point of view of the problem of Israel.

2 - *Beyond Occupation*, Rosemary Ruether and Marc Ellis
This collection of articles written from the perspective of Jews, Christians and Palestinians was an eye-opener for me. It pulled me into the pain of the occupation and its tragic cost in human dignity and life.

3 - *Blood Brothers*, Elias Chacour
This book by a Palestinian priest of the Galilee reads like a novel as he tells of his struggle against hate during his spiritual pilgrimage under the Israeli domination of his land. Chacour amazes me with his love for both Jews and Palestinians. This book also gave me an inside picture of what really happened to the Palestinians in 1948.

4 - *From Beirut to Jerusalem*, Thomas Freedman
I found that Thomas Freedman, a Jewish correspondent for The *New York Times* and reporter living in Beirut and Jerusalem, gives a balanced account of Middle East history. This popular book is easy reading and a good place to begin for those who are open to reading history with their emotions. However, there is another book entitled, *From Beirut to Jerusalem* written by Dr. Swee Chai Ang. She was on duty in the hospital in Sabra and Shatila during the massacres of 1982 and she writes from her emotions. This book is not published in the U.S.A., but can be obtained from Americans for Middle East Understanding, Room 241, 475 Riverside Drive, New York, NY. 10115.

5 - *The End of Zionism*, eibie Weizfeld
This anthology by Jewish writers proclaims that Zionism is an idea whose time has gone. These writers bring into question the blind assumption that modern Zionism has a biblical and moral basis in history. This little book points out the resistance, especially expressed by American Jews, to Zionism as the solution to the Jewish problem.

6 - *The Hidden History of Zionism*, Ralph Schoenman

As Executive Director of the Bertrand Russell Peace Foundation, Schoenman had negotiated with numerous heads of state for the release of political prisoners. His heartfelt concern for the abuse of human beings stirred me emotionally as I read his book. He documents unbelievable atrocities committed by the Israeli government. This is a harsh book and it made me angry.

7 - *A Compassionate Peace*, Everett Mendelsohn

This book, sponsored by The American Friends Service Committee, is a common sense account of the Middle East problem. It reads like a handbook on the causes and cures for peace in the Middle East. Its Jewish writer holds true to his stated theme of compassion for all people.

8 - *Anti-Zionism*, Roselle Tekiner, Samir Abed-Rabbo, and Norton Mezvinsky.

This collection of essays challenges the idea that many of us have held that Israel is a peace-seeking democratic nation. These writers point out that Zionism, rather than being a cure for Jewish ills, is in fact the number one culprit in the destruction of peaceful relations between Jews and the other peoples of the Middle East.

9 - *Prophesy and Politics*, Grace Halsell

Having taken two Holy Land trips with Jerry Falwell, Halsell unpacks the commitment of certain fundamentalists to "Armageddon Theology" which seeks to biblically justify Israel's expansionism by proclaiming it as the will of God. This easy-to-read book is a must for anyone seeking to balance the biases of the early Old Testament tribal god with the God of universal love proclaimed by the later prophets and the writers of the New Testament.

10- *Arafat*, Alan Hart

I learned as much about Arafat's era in this book as I learned about Yasser Arafat. It shows the context for his passion for a Palestinian homeland and the stages of his development in searching for a diplomatic peace. This book helped me to better understand the Palestinians, the PLO and the ultimate question about Arafat...Terrorist or Peacemaker?

11 - *Deliberate Deceptions*, Paul Findley

This easy to read account of the facts and fallacies of the U.S.-Israeli relationship is a good up-to-date companion piece to Simon Flapan's out of print book listed above. Paul Findley is a former U.S. Representative from Illinois who has dedicated his post-government days to examining the truth about U.S. involvement with Israel. This book helped me to again realize how much propaganda is accepted as truth and how painful it is for so many in the Middle East to examine accepted beliefs.

12 - *The Passionate Attachment*, George W. Ball and Douglas B. Ball.

This former Under Secretary of State and U.N. Ambassador and his son have researched the history of four decades of U.S. involvement in the web of Middle East politics. They examine the moral and financial cost of this one-sided, irrational attachment and show its destructiveness to the people of America, Palestine and Israel.

I also recommend several magazines:

1 - *The Washington Report on Middle East Affairs*, P.O. Box 53062, Washington, D.C. 20009 ($19) is published by the American Education Trust, a non-profit foundation incorporated by retired U.S. foreign service officials, former U.S. ambassadors, governmental officials and members of Congress. *The Washington Report* contains a dozen articles each month judged to be consistent with the United Nations' resolutions, concerns for human rights, self-determination and fair play. It provides an up-to-date fact-filled resource of Middle East history, policy and current events. This one is a must.

2 - *The Link* is published bimonthly by Americans for Middle East Understanding, Inc., Room 241, 475 Riverside Drive, New York, N.Y. 10115 ($25). This 16-page special usually features a single article focusing on one major subject. I have also found its listings of books and videos at discount prices most helpful.

3 - *Breaking the Siege* is published by Middle East Justice Network, P.O. Box 558, Cambridge, Mass. 02239 (Donation). This short 8-page magazine reflects the commitments of Americans drawn together by a common concern about our government's role in supporting the Israeli occupation of the West Bank and Gaza. This newsletter supports U.N. resolution 242, and the principle of "land for peace,"

leading toward the creation of Palestine and a "two state solution."

4 - *Challenge*, P.O. Box 14338, Tel Aviv, 61142, Israel ($30) This 42-page bimonthly is published in Jerusalem. Its articles are written by Arabs and Jews representing the Israeli left.

5 - *Sojourners*, Box 29277, Washington, D.C. 20078-5290 ($27). Subtitled Faith, Politics and Culture, *Sojourners* seeks to present voices of conscience addressing issues from a position of Christian faith.

6 - *Tikkun*, P.O. Box 332, Mt. Morris, Ill. 61054-0332 ($30) is a bimonthly Jewish critique of politics, culture and society. I read this magazine because of my respect for Michael Lerner, its editor and a Jewish writer who seeks Israel's security in accountability.

7 - *Commonweal*, 15 Dutch Street, New York, N.Y. 10038 ($36). This bimonthly is a review of public affairs from a religious perspective.

8 - *The Lamplight*, published by Local Alliance for Mideast Peace, 220 Carrick Street, Ste. 223A, Knoxville, Tenn. 37921. This short newsletter seeks "illumination on the Middle East." It's free, but contributions are appreciated. It's editor, Ken Schubert, and many of its featured writers are Jewish.

9 - *Lies of Our Times*, 142 West 4th Street, New York, N.Y. 10012 ($24) is a magazine of media criticism.

10 - *Middle East International*, 1700 17th Street, NW, Washington, D.C. 20009, Quarterly ($59).

We Can Listen To Those Who Know

Most cities offer just such opportunities. But no matter where you live, somewhere within driving distance someone is speaking out for justice. I recommend getting in touch with such groups as:

1 - Mercy Corps, an international group committed to helping the poor and oppressed. Through a Mid-East newsletter, Mercy Corps seeks to educate the public about the plight of the oppressed and motivate works for peace. In addition to a Mid-East newsletter, this agency sponsors several fact-finding study trips to the Middle East every year. For information, write: Don Wagner, Director of the Middle East

Program, Mercy Corps International, 175 W. Jackson Blvd., Suite 1800, Chicago, Ill. 60604.

2 - Palestinian Human Rights Information Center, 4753 North Broadway, Suite 930, Chicago, Ill. 60640, is an American organization with offices in Israel, focusing exclusively on the struggle of the Palestinian people and works through non-violent, peaceful means. PHRIC seeks to gain release of political prisoners, obtain medical care for wounded Palestinians and educate the public through written materials and speakers.

3 - The American Alliance for Palestinian Human Rights, 2435 Virginia Ave. NW, Washington, D.C. 20037 issues monthly bulletins for immediate concern and action. This is a good resource for statistics.

4 - Middle East Council of Churches, P.O. Box 4259, Limasol, Cyprus, publishes a News Report and Perspective ($25).

You may have to do some detective work to find them, but resources and opportunities to learn the other side are there for anyone willing to look for them. In many cases, being informed is only a phone call away.

It's not enough for a church to pray for peace. Prayer alone is insufficient. Any church that relies on rhetoric rather than taking a stand against human oppression not only creates a smoke screen, it denies its own theology. People are suffering as we pray. To them, there is no time to waste. I remember speaking to a group in my church about injustice to the Palestinians when one of my elders said, "But Tom, it's just going to take time."

"How much time?" I asked.

"It might take another hundred years." he responded, trying to sound like a prophet.

But the Palestinians don't have a hundred years.

We Can Re-Study the Bible

If it's true that you can't step in the same river twice, then it's equally true that you can't really re-read the Bible. The context and the reader are constantly changing. The words may be the same, but the reading relates to a different situation. That is exactly what is happening to me. I am not the same person I was when I read it last. Life pulls me away from where I first began my Bible study. How can I

166

know about the horrible pain of life in which so many suffer, and still read the Bible as though it's a bit of inspirational material to help me build my self esteem and feel good about God? How can I continue to think that the main message of the Bible is focused on my personal salvation when so many of God's people continue to live this life in squalor?

Re-reading the Bible pulls us into a dialogue with the God who all the way through the Bible sided with the oppressed. If we resist at first, its only natural, because:

> It is appropriate that anyone's first reaction to the "good news" should be to find it bad news, because the condition of receiving the good news is *change* (what the Bible calls *metanoia,* "conversion"). To be told that we need to change is to be told that we are presently unsatisfactory. So the admonition to change is always bad news, making us uncomfortable and defensive.[1]

We Can Attend a Peace Conference

Every church denomination I know offers an assembly-wide peace conference every year. The experience of gathering with hundreds of other Christians who share the same concerns about what is happening in the world gives a tremendous amount of information and an emotional boost to those struggling to be peacemakers. At the conference I attended last year, I heard speakers, including Palestinians, from Israel and the occupied territories. I experienced group workshops led by informed church leaders, and met in small groups to share feelings and frustrations. It helped me to learn, in a group of 37 people, that there were 17 other ministers, and every one admitted that they were in *"trouble back home"* with their local congregations because of their criticism of Israel. "It's not what you are trying to do, Reverend, it's the way you are going about it," we had all been told.

II. WE CAN FIND WAYS TO SHOW SOLIDARITY

I purchased a stole when I was in Israel. I bought it primarily to give a little income to the Palestinians who had made it. But by the time I got home, that stole had taken on meaning for me. At first I thought of it as a mourning shawl for the suffering and death of the Palestinians. Now, a year later, I wear it every time I preach to declare solidarity with the Palestinians.

Solidarity involves knowing and feeling the heartbeat of those in the Christian church in Israel. Solidarity is what Paul had in mind when he said, "If one member suffers, all suffer together..." (I Corinthians 12:26). I have never looked over my shoulder or up on the roof tops when I went to church and seen armed soldiers of another faith who acted as though they hated me, but I can imagine how frightening that must be. From Bethlehem to Jerusalem, soldiers with guns and binoculars watch Christians and Muslims as they gather to worship and study. Palestinians are subject to harassment, humiliation and beatings by Israeli soldiers every time they step out of the house.

The more than 140,000 native-born Christians living in Israel, linked with the 10,000 or so from abroad who work in the Christian hospitals, study in Christian schools, and pilgrimage from abroad, form a kinship with the Christians of America. We share faith and history all the way back to the day of Pentecost. And they, those indigenous Christians of Israel, mold our imagination of what it's like to be Christians under occupation.

"When I step out of the door," one Jerusalem pastor said, "I see soldiers pushing young Arab boys to the wall and kicking their groins. It makes it kind of hard to appreciate the Zionist dream."

"Rather than God favoring the Jews," an Episcopalian priest said, "He, in fact, favors the Palestinians. The God of the Bible always supports the weak against the strong." Of course, I feel a close bond to those Palestinians who are Christians. That is why I write primarily with the Christian reader in mind. At the same time, we must recognize that by far, most Palestinians are Muslims, who are also the children of God with whom I must claim solidarity. Solidarity works both ways. I can learn from the Christians in Israel. They call me to Christ-like attitudes in the face of oppression. They force me to examine the depth of my own commitment as I witness their faith and hope.

Al Haq

Another way I can express solidarity is by joining Al Haq. This organization of legal professionals with experience in interpreting international law documents the abuse of human rights in the occupied territories. They operate the only law library available to Palestinians in the West Bank and seek to hold Israel accountable to her own professed "democratic" standards.

Of Al Haq, the *Christian Century* says:

> While it has been fairly successful in intervening for visa applications, it finds that attaining family reunification or preventing torture and house demolitions is much more difficult. A cadre of fieldworkers who live where they work makes Al Haq one of the most comprehensive and reliable documenters of human rights abuses. Although international visibility has given Al Haq a degree of security, some fieldworkers have been detained and tortured by the Israeli Defense Forces.[2]

In the summer of 1991, I visited the office of Al Haq in Ramallah and listened to one of their directors tell of their frustrating efforts to protect Palestinians from abuse. She became emotional when she told of Israeli torture. Even though she told us nothing that we had not already heard many times by many different people, to hear it from a spokesperson of Al Haq, the human rights organization that had just received the Carter-Menil Human Rights Prize from former President Jimmy Carter, reconfirmed how rampant and senseless this evil has become.

"But why?" Someone from our group asked, "Why would Israel want to torture people for no reason?"

"Israel tortures just to make life here unbearable. Israel wants us out of here, to leave our land. That's the reason for so many deportations. Do you know about deportations?" she asked. "When women and children are deported, soon, the fathers leave also. That means fewer Palestinians. It's a form of expulsion." It has become commonplace to pack up women without residency cards and, with only minutes notice, expel them across the border.

Al Haq reports:

> In 1967, many Palestinians were forced to leave the country. The Zionists issued orders - anyone who was out of the country or had left the area could not return, even though the

family lived here. Palestinian ID cards allow you to work, but you are not a citizen. You are "illegal" unless you have an Israeli ID card.[3]

An Al Haq worker went on to explain:

Until September 9, 1987, any child born here could be registered on the father's ID. It is an Arab tradition that the children are identified by the father, not the mother. Israel never cared about it. But suddenly, Israel issued an executive order. Any child born here may be legally registered only in the mother's ID. So, if the mother doesn't have an ID, if she is from Jordan or the US or Europe and she is married to a Palestinian, she is not permitted to stay. Her child, even though born here, is considered a foreigner and not a legal resident. In 1989, the Israelis deported 150 women from the West Bank because they didn't have proper ID cards. They send her pre-1987 children with her because they too are "illegal,"leaving the father with the younger children. It's only a matter of time before the father leaves too.[4]

Separating families violates one of the most basic human rights recognized by the world community.

How can we help?

Adopt-a-Family

Al Haq will assist anyone willing to adopt a separated family. This means that you choose to become an advocate for a particular family seeking reunification. You can even adopt a doctor, professor, engineer or a member of any particular profession if you happen to share that in common. To get started, Al Haq will make the link and will send you case histories and information on several families. Then, you choose. The goal is to persuade the Israeli authorities to reconsider their policy toward reunification in general and toward your family in particular. You write the Israeli authorities, citing your concern for their violation of international law. You may also write your family. Publicity helps. Solidarity encourages.

Write Al Haq, P.O. Box 1413, Ramallah, West Bank, Israel, and say that you want to help stop Israel from separating families. Or you could make a financial contribution.

Responsible Tourism

"When the scuds hit Israel, Jews from all over America poured in by the thousands. They brought money, love and understanding support. Many Christians came with them bringing prayers, sympathy and pledges of America's unfailing support. But nobody," a Christian in the West Bank said, "Nobody brought a caring word to the Palestinians, not even to the Christian Palestinians. Where was the church?"

I spoke with the pastor of a small Christian congregation in the Galilee that struggles to understand why American Christians are generally more supportive of the Jewish state that persecutes the church than of the Christians who share our faith. "How can our brothers and sisters in Christ let their government do this to us?" they ask.

"I am a pastor," another said. "What can I say to the mother of a child whose arms have been deliberately broken by uniformed Israeli soldiers? Don't Christians in American care? Do they even know that we exist?"

My mind immediately recalled a brochure I had received in the mail a few weeks earlier:

FOR THE GREATEST SPIRITUAL EXPERIENCE OF YOUR LIFE
COME WITH US
WALK WHERE JESUS WALKED

The pastor of a large suburban church was recruiting passengers for a "Holy Land Trip." Of course, he gets one free trip for every five paying passengers he recruits. The brochure told of the places they would see: the Garden tomb, where they would have a Communion Service, the Via Dolorosa, the Mount of Olives and the Garden of Gethsemane, the Sea of Galilee and the hillside where Jesus preached the Sermon on the Mount. It was to be the spiritual experience of a lifetime. Then the brochure added several "unique" opportunities that the group would have to gain a better understanding of the miracle of the State of Israel, including a visit to Yad Vashem, an absorption center for Soviet and Ethiopian Jews rescued by Israel, the Knesset, and numerous war memorials in honor of Israeli war heroes.

There was not one mention in the entire brochure of making contact with Christian Palestinians or anything else that was of Christianity and alive. Having led such tours, I am confident that everyone on the trip will come home feeling sorry for the mistreated Jews of Israel and pledge their support to the betterment of Jewish life in Israel, as I once did.

Travel if you can, but go with Mercy Corps or your denomination's Peace Group who will introduce you to the occupied territories and allow you to meet, talk and pray with some Palestinian Christians.

III. WE CAN FIND WAYS TO
SPEAK OUR CONCERNS

Speak up for the Palestinians and you will make enemies. Yet, as Christians, we must be willing to raise issues that until now we have chosen to dodge. We must risk disagreement with some good people who because they are pro-Zionist Jews, have Jewish friends, or are unwilling to challenge old misconceptions, have in the past refused to deal with the Palestinian issue. No longer can we tolerate the silence, even by some wonderful friends who do not want to see Israel judged by the same criterion as are applied to the U.S. or other regimes.

Some good people who have done great work on apartheid in South Africa are unwilling to speak about the connection— military, economic, even nuclear—between South Africa and Israel. Some who supported the civil rights movement with their influence and money to prevent discrimination against African-Americans will support the most blatant racism in Israel. There are anti-nuclear movement people who have not opened their mouths to address Israel's arsenal of over 200 nuclear bombs. Many decry injustice in Central America, but say nothing about the horrors in Palestine.

Maybe, out of fear of anti-Semitism, and in the name of expiation for sins of the past – the shame of the holocaust — we remain silent in face of a holocaust on Palestinians. There seems to be an unspoken agreement. Some issues are simply not raised, some matters not addressed; the evils of Israel are not admissible. That day must be over. We must find a way to speak out on the issue of peace and justice. We must beat the taboo.

In my church, we have had an adult Sunday School class study *Justice and Only Justice;* another invited informed

Arab Americans to speak and answer questions. In the interest of "balance," we have heard pro-Israel speakers. But the Zionist side has been promoted for 43 years. It's a new thing to give a little hearing to the Palestinian side.

We Can Speak to Political Leaders
My friend Paul said, "I will vote. All I can do is vote." I disagree. Where is the Christian witness in going into a booth, once every couple of years, pulling the curtain and casting a private vote? That's the least we can do. Paul also has a voice. He can speak to friends and to politicians, and he can write letters. Politicians are impressed by personal letters. The magic words are, "I am a constituent." Anyone who takes the time to write a personal letter will get a hearing. Letters, far more effective than post cards or petitions, get counted.

Politicians may not always answer concerns, but they are always influenced by personal letters. Even better are visits to their offices. Few politicians will ignore the interests of anyone who cares enough about an issue to make a personal visit. Names, addresses, voting records and committee responsibilities can be found in the local library, or in such books as: *The Almanac of American Politics*, published annually. (See Bibliography)

We Can Listen With Our Hearts
Listen to Jonathan Kuttab, civil rights leader and cofounder of Al Haq, as he talks in the summer of 1991 about the source of Palestinian hope:

> But I tell you, all is not lost. Quite the contrary. There are many new and excellent signs for hope. For you see, we Palestinians have been through many very difficult times before. We hung in there, not because we were confident that we have more military power, more financial resources, more powerful friends, but because of a deep and abiding faith in the sovereignty of God, that God exists, that he is a God of justice and of peace, and that evil cannot prevail forever.

As I listened to Jonathan Kuttab, preaching at a church conference in 1991, I was humbled to hear this Palestinian, demeaned all his life by Jews, condemn anti-Semitism.

173

In all love, there is still anti-semitism in this country. Anti-Jewish anti-semitism. The church must be careful. We must continue to be opposed to racism and discrimination no matter against who or by whom it is exercised. We must not allow ourselves to fall into the easy trap of appealing to anti-Jewish sentiments, because it is out there. Our approach must be based on our faith and love. We must be willing to seek peace out of love for Palestinians and Jews.

Listening to this faithful Christian of the occupied territories humbled me. As I walked with Palestinians through the squalor of the West Bank and Gaza, the question that almost choked me was, "Where is God?" When I saw the powerlessness of Palestinians and the ruthless might of Israel, my gut feeling was one of despair. The spirit of a Jonathan Kuttab amazes me. I learned about the meaning of faith from this Palestinian Christian from Ramallah.

Another Jerusalem Christian from whom I learned about the meaning of faith is Father M. This Roman Catholic priest does not minimize the arrogance of Israeli power. Father M. lives in Jerusalem and offers his services in the occupied territories visiting the sick, attending the people in prison, and doing relief work in the refugee camps. M. says:

> It's the knock at the door at two in the morning that is the threatening part of living in a camp. People disappear. Or people go to prison. Or they are held for eighteen days incommunicado. They have no basic rights.[5]

M. goes on to describe the despair of Palestinian humiliation:

> If you take all of the Palestinians who have been killed, the number is roughly around 1,000. The number who have required medical attention is roughly around 106,000. The over 50,000 who have been in prison, the houses that have been demolished, the thousands of trees that have been uprooted, the deportations. You take all of the statistics together. Just take an average. What it averages out to is that *every Palestinian family has had at least two members that have either been killed, deported, arrested or tortured.*
>
> In the camps, the people ask in the evenings together: for what? For what?

Yet, Father M. continues to see Christ in the midst of their despair:

> There are times, I feel, in the camp when the people demon-
> strate by their life that there is a certain kind of awareness.
> Sometimes it is hard to even put it into words. They touch
> and feel the presence of Christ in the camps. There were
> times when I felt it more there than at any other place. It's
> eerie. I can remember one particular night, sitting in a small
> room. We went to visit this family. It was in the winter and
> the boy from the family was 21 years old and had been de-
> ported. When someone is deported, you should know that
> the Palestinians are usually taken by helicopter into an area
> of Lebanon where the people are not friendly towards Pales-
> tinians and are usually left there and the helicopters take
> off. They quickly run and hide and hope to find somewhere to
> get protection. We were in this home this night, spending time
> with the family and there was nothing there but the lantern
> and that was supplying the light and the heat. And t h e r e
> was a kind of a quietness there, and in the midst...the best
> way I can describe it, was "the presence of Christ." People
> seem to know it without saying a word. You could just feel it.
> And then we left.

And I learned about forgiveness from the Peacemaker,
Elias Chacour, speaking from his school in the Galilee:

> We consider Palestine our homeland. We were unable to con-
> vince the West that we belong to Palestine but we never hated
> the Jews. We will never hate. Never. Ever. Because simply, as
> I teach our students, "Hatred is corruption." If you are hated,
> the worst thing that can happen to you is to give back hate
> for hate. We don't fear the Jews and we will never hate them.
> But we do not agree with them. To take our homes, our land,
> to deprive us of all our human rights, our human dignity, pro-
> testing that they were persecuted somewhere else, for you
> see, they are afraid. We understand their fear. But we can't
> understand their expression of these fears by persecuting us.

CONCLUSION

In spite of the fact that Christians in Israel feel a special
calling to remain in the land of the mother church, tensions
orchestrated by the Israeli military make it harder to hold
on. Pressure to leave includes attacks on clergy, arson in the

burning of church buildings, desecration of church property and cemeteries, and withholding of travel visas. When Israel goes on record as desiring to be a purely Jewish state, she means it.

"My church is losing membership," Na'im Ateek said to me. "Almost everywhere you look, Christians are leaving. And I don't blame them."

Gabriel Habib, General Secretary of the Middle East Council of Churches, said:

> Fear, human suffering, and hopelessness have caused so many Christians to emigrate that there is profound concern about the very continuity of Christian presence and witness in this region.[6]

In 1922, over half of the 28,452 inhabitants of Jerusalem were Christians. Half a century later, the number had dropped to less than ten percent of that number. Today, Christians in Jerusalem number around 6,000. According to Donald Wagner of *Mercy Corps*:

> Harder hit than Jerusalem are Ramallah and Bethlehem on the West Bank. When Israel was established in 1948, these cities were overwhelmingly Christian. Today, due to political and economic turmoil, over half the Christians have left for Europe or North or South America. More Palestinian Christians from Ramallah live in Detroit and in Jacksonville, Florida, than in Ramallah. More Palestinian Christians from Bethlehem live in Chile and Brazil than in their homeland.[7]

Some Christian leaders even predict that the church in Israel under the present situation cannot survive more than a decade or two. Some say the church in Jerusalem may soon become no more than a museum for western pilgrims.

While Holy Land Christians have cause to worry about their survival, many American Christians also have cause to worry about the quality of our faith. I remember Father Chacour's words when someone asked how the American church might help him.

"Help?" he said. "I need no help. I am seeking my life's work within the will of God."

"But, when we go home," she said. "We all have a need to do something."

"Then pray." he said. "Pray for yourselves." Then he added with a voice of concern a statement that cut me where I am very sensitive. *"The church in America,"* he said, *"has lost its soul."*[8]

As a pastor for thirty years, I live with the fear that he is right. To take up a cross and follow the carpenter into self-denial for the uplifting of the oppressed is not our style. When I claim solidarity with the Palestinians, I do it as much for my own faith as for them.

In this book, I have attempted to show the other side of Israel in the light of Liberation Theology. My interest is not in condemning Israel, but in calling Israel to a responsible use of power which is not only in keeping with Judaism, but may be her only hope of survival. My other interest is in calling American Christians into responsible discipleship, which is our hope of survival.

There is also hope in the multitude of Jews around the whole world who take seriously their own theology and will endeavor to direct Israel toward becoming a leading nation morally as well as politically.

And there is hope in the God of Justice and Compassion proclaimed and worshipped by Jew, Muslim and Christian.

NOTES

Introduction

1- Jack G. Shaheen, *The T.V. Arab,* (Bowling Green: Bowling Green State University Popular Press, 1984), p. 38.
2- Naim Ateek, *Justice, and Only Justice,* (Maryknoll, New York: Orbis Books, 1989), p.36.
3 - *Ibid.,* p.32.
4 - *Ibid.,* p.46.
5 - Statement by the Heads of the Christian Communities in Jerusalem, April 26, 1989.

Chapter One - Human Rights as Official Policy

1 - Private conversations with a minister, recently returned from Israel-Palestine and with a doctor while attending a conference of Churches for Middle East Peace, Washington, D.C., May 13-15, 1990. If there had not surfaced in the meantime so much collaborating evidence of similar accounts, I would have written them off as hyperbole.
2 - Rosemary Radford Ruether and Marc H. Ellis, *Beyond Occupation,* (Boston: Beacon press. 1990), p.1.
3 - The Newsletter of the Middle East Justice Network, *Breaking the Siege,* Vol 3, No.2, June-July 1991, p.6.
4 - Paul Findley, *Deliberate Deceptions, Facing the Facts About the U.S.-Israeli Relationship* (Brooklyn, NY, Lawrence Hill Books, 1993), p.xi.
5 - Amnesty International, *Israel and the Occupied Territories,* 1990.
6 - The Database Project on Palestine Human Rights, *The Cost of Freedom.* 1988 A Special Report , p.6.
7 - *Ibid.* p.6.
8 - "Rights Group Accuses Israel of Violence Against Children in Palestinian Uprising," *Washington Post,* May 17, 1990
9 - *Ibid.*
10- *Ibid.*
11- *Cost of Freedom* p.13.
12- *Ibid.,* p.9.
13- Rights Group Accuses Israel of Violence Against Children in Palestinian Uprising, *Washington Post.* May 17, 1990
14- *Newsweek,* February 8, 1988. p.33.
15- Ralph Schoenman, *The Hidden History of Zionism,* (Santa Barbara, Ca.: Veritas Press, 1988), p.3.
16- Rights Group Accuses Israel of Violence Against Children in Palestinian Uprising, *Washington Post,* May 17, 1990
17- *Ibid.,* p.72.

18- Schoenman, *Op. cit.,* p.71.

19- *Sunday Times,* London, June 19, 1977.

20- Schoenman, *Op. cit.,* p.78.

21- Thomas L. Friedman, *From Beirut to Jerusalem,* (New York: Farrar Straus Giroux, 1988), p.357.

22- *Cost of Freedom,* p.21.

23- Private conversation with a Roman Catholic priest in Jerusalem, July 9, 1991, recorded by the author.

24- Wesley G. Pippert, *Land of Promise, Land of Strife,* (Waco, Texas: Word Books, 1988), p.100.

25- *Cost of Freedom,* p. 31.

26- *Ibid.,* p.32.

27- *Ibid.,* p.18.

28- Pippert, *Op. cit.,* p.115.

29- Mendelsohn, *Op. cit.,* p.33.

30- Conversation with a Roman Catholic priest recorded in Jerusalem on July 9, 1991. I have been made aware of the risk he runs in speaking critically of Israel. I have heard of one source being beaten to death by Israeli soldiers a few days after his name was used as a reference. Therefore while recognizing that it weaken my claim to credibility, through this book, I have chosen to hold some names of sources in confidence.

31- Editorial: James M. Wall, *The Christian Century*, November 8, 1989.

32- Ze'ev Schiff and Ehud Ya'ari, *Intifada,* (New York: Simon and Schuster, 1990), p.97.

33- Mendelsohn, *op. cit.,* p.52.

34- Editorial: James M. Wall, *The Christian Century*, November 8, 1989.

35- *Ibid.*

36- Middle East Justice Network, Action Alert, #17, 1A March 22, 1990.

37- Associated Press, *Atlanta Constitution*, April 23, 1990.

38- Mendelsohn, *op. cit.,* pp.45-49.

39- The 200th General Assembly (1988) of the Presbyterian Church (USA).

Chapter Two - Jacob: The Dark Side of David

1- Elias Chacour, *Blood Brothers,* (Old Tappan, N.J. Chosen Books, Fleming H. Revell, 1984.) p.121.

2 - Erskine Childers, *The Other Exodus;* Spectator, London. May 12, 1961; reprinted in Walter Laqueur and Barry Rubin, eds, *The Arab-Israeli Reader: a Documentary History of the Middle East Conflict,* Penguin, 1984, Document 34. Cited, Clifford A. Wright, *Facts and Fables: The Arab- Israeli Conflict,* (London: Kegan Paul International, 1989), p.14.

3 - *Ibid.,* p.14.

4 - Quoted in David Hirst, *The Gun and the Olive Branch: The Roots of Violence in the Middle East,* Faber and Faber, 1977, p.141. Cited,

NOTES

Clifford A. Wright, *Facts and Fables: The Arab-Israeli Conflict*, (London: Kegan Paul International, 1989), p.19.

5 - From Benzion Dinur, ed., *Sefer Toldot Ha-Haganah* (8 vols.) Zionist Library-Marakot, 1954-72, III, p.1253-5, appendix 398, p.1939-43 (The Official History of the Haganah, unpublished in English. Cited, Clifford A.Wright, *Facts and Fables: The Arab-Israeli Conflict*, (London: Kegan Paul International, 1989), p.17.

6 - Cited in Lenni Brenner, *The Iron Wall: Zionist Revolution From Jabotinsky to Shamir*, (London, Zed Books, Ltd. 1984), p.97. Quoted by Ralph Schoenman, *The Hidden History of Zionism*, (Santa Barbara, California: Veritas Press, 1988), p.33.

7 - Alan Hart, *Arafat, Terrorist or Peacemaker*, (London: Sidgwick and Jackson, 1984), p.53.

8 - Television Special, A&E Premier, *Terror, A Three part Investigation of Political Violence,* Part One: A Fundamental Conflict. Jack Perkins, Narrator; Film Archives. Israeli Television in Movitone, UNRWA, VISNEWS, Produced by Tony Stark, aired Channel 8 and 30, Atlanta, Georgia, March, 1991.

9 - David K. Shipler, *Arab and Jew,* (New York: Penguin Books, 1968), p.40.

10- Ralph Schoenman. *The Hidden History of Zionism,* (Santa Barbara, California: Veritas Press, 1988), p.34.

11- Livia Rokach, *Israel's Sacred Terrorism,* (Belmont, Massachusetts: Association of Arab-American Graduates, Inc. 1986), p.XIX.

12- *Ibid.*, p.XIX.

13- *Time Magazine*, October 4, 1982. Cited in Schoenman, *op. cit.,* p.65.

14- Schoenman, *op. cit.,* p.66.

15- *Ibid.*, p.67.

16- *Ibid.*, p.4.

17- *Ibid.*, p.4-5.

18- *Ibid.*, p.4.

19- Chacour, *op. cit.,* p.122.

20- Shiha Flapan, *The Birth of Israel*, (New York: Pantheon Books, 1987), p.71.

21- *Ibid.*, p.71.

22- Fred J. Khouri, *The Arab Israeli Dilema, Third Edition,* (Syracuse, N.Y.: Syracuse University Press, 1985), p.77.

23- *Ibid.*, p.72.

24- *Ibid.*, p.77.

25- Schoenman, *op. cit.,* p.33.

26- *Ibid.*, p.33.

27- *Ibid.*, p.112.

28- *Ibid.*, p.31.

29- *Ibid.*, p.31.

30- *Ibid.*, p.35.

31- *Ibid.*, p.113.

32- *Ibid.*, p.114.
33- *Ibid.*, p.116.
34- *Ibid.*, p.59.

Chapter Three - Arguments/Counter Arguments

1 - Jacobo Timerman, *The Longest War*, (New York: Alfred A. Knopf, 1982), p.158.
2 - Rosemary Radford Ruether and Marc H. Ellis, *Beyond Occupation*, (Boston: Beacon Press, 1990), p.17.
3 - Marc H. Ellis, *Beyond Innocence and Redemption,* (San Francisco: Harper and Row Publishers, 1990), p.73.
4 - *Ibid.* p.74.
5 - Ruether and Ellis, *op. cit.,* p.19.
6 - *Ibid.* p.99.
7 - *Ibid.* p.100.
8 - *Ibid.* p.55.
9 - *Ibid.* p.80.
10- *Ibid.* p.82.
11- Paul A. Hopkins, "Facing the Charge of Anti-Semitism," *The Link,* Vol. 25, No. 1, January/March 1992. p.1
12- Jon Carroll, "On Being Called an Anti-Semite," *The Washington Report on Middle East Affairs,* December-January 1992, p.53
13- Ruether and Ellis, *op. cit.,* pp. 65-66.
14 -*Ibid.* p.68.
15 - Naim Ateek, *Justice, and Only Justice,* (Maryknoll, N.Y.: Orbis Books, 1989), p.136.
16 - The Database Project on Palestine Human Rights, *The Cost of Freedom.* 1988 A Special Report p.5.
17 - Ruether and Ellis, *op. cit.,* p.236
18 - *Ibid.*, p.244.
19 - Thomas L. Friedman, *From Beirut to Jerusalem,* (New York: Farrar Straus Giroux, 1988), p.353.
20 - Colin Chapman, *Whose Promised Land.*, (Batavia, Illinois: Lion International Paperback, 1983), p.179.
21 - *Ibid.*, p.180.

Chapter Four - Religion and Politics must Mix

1 - Edward M. Plass, *What Luther Says, An Anthology,* (Saint Louis, Missouri: Concordia Publishing House, 1959), Volume I, p.294.
2 - *Ibid.*, p.296.
3 - *Ibid.*, p.292.
4 - William M. Ramsey, *The Wall of Separation,* (Louisville: The Westminster/John Knox Press, 1989), p.30.

NOTES

5 - Edwin Robertson, *The Shame and the Sacrifice,* (New York: Macmillian Publishing Company, 1988) p.76.

6 - *Ibid.,* p.148.

7 - *Ibid.,* p.117.

8 - Ronald H. Stone, ed., *Reformed Faith and Politics,* (Washington, D.C.: The University Press of America, 1983), p.161.

9 - John J. Ansbro, *Martin Luther King, Jr.,; The Making of a Mind.,* (Maryknoll, N.Y.: Orbis Books, 1982), p. 66. 10 - Taylor Branch, *Parting the Waters: America in the King Years, 1954-1963,* (New York: Simon and Schuster, 1988), p.141.

11 - Martin Luther King Jr. Sermon preached at Dexter Avenue Baptist Church, Montgomery, Alabama. Christmas 1957.

12 - Martin Luther King, Jr. Sermon, *The Future of Integration,* January 19, 1968.

13 - Martin Luther King, Jr., *Why We Can't Wait.,* (New York: Harper and Row, 1963), p.80.

14 -Martin Luther King, Jr., Sermon, *Our God is Marching On,* Preached, March 25, 1965.

15 - Ramsey, *Op.cit.,* p.1.

16 - *Ibid.,* p.3.

17 - *Ibid.,* p.4.

18 - *Ibid.,* p.36.

19 -Maurice W. Armstrong, Lefferts A. Loetcher, and Charles A. Anderson, eds., *The Presbyterian Enterprise: Source of American Presbyterian History,* (Louisville: The Westminster Press, 1961), p. 215.

20 - James H. Cone, *God of the Oppressed,* (New York: Harper and Row, San Francisco, 1975), p.49.

21 - Minutes: 105th General Assembly of the Presbyterian Church in the United States, (Atlanta: Office of the General Assembly., 1965) p. 41 Cited in Thomas L. Are, Jr. *Violence and the Influence of Theological Anthropology in the Theology of Malcolm X, Martin Luther King, Jr., and James H. Cone,* (A Thesis Submitted in Partial Fulfillment of the Requirements for the Degree of Master of Sacred Theology, Yale University Divinity School, New Haven, Connecticut, 1990), p. 51.

22 - See Ezekiel 38:3.

Chapter Five - Liberation Theology and the State of Israel

1 - Phillip Berryman, *Liberation Theology,* (Pantheon Books, a Division of Random House, New York, 1987) p. 43.

2 - *Ibid.,* p.101.

3 - *Ibid.,* p.3.

4 - I am indebted to Robert McAfee Brown and his book *Unexpected News* for his interpretation of the Exodus story related here. Robert McAfee Brown, *Unexpected News, Reading the Bible with Third World Eyes,* (Westminster Press, Philadelphia, Pa. 1984).

5 - *Ibid.,* p.40

6 - Colin Chapman, *Whose Promised Land,* (Tring - Batavia - Sydney, Lion International, 1983), p.101.

7 - *Ha'aretz,* July 5, 1982. Cited in Clifford A. Wright, *Facts and Fables: The Arab-Israeli Conflict.* (New York: Kegan Paul International, 1989). p.167.

8 - Lecture by Marc Ellis, June 10, 1991, Atlanta, Georgia, recorded by the author.

9 - Robert McAfee Brown, *Christians in the West,* cited in Ruether and Ellis, *op. cit.,* p.146

Chapter Six - How Israel Influences America

1 - Richard H. Curtiss, *Stealth PACs: How Israel's American Lobby seeks to Control U.S. Middle East Policy,* (Washington, D.C.: American Educational Trust, 1990), p.15.

2 - *Ibid.*, p.vi.

3 - Copyrights 1985, 1989 by Paul Findley, *They Dare to Speak Out: People and Institutions Confront Israel's Lobby,* p. 76. All exerpts reprinted by permission of the publisher, Lawrence Hill Books, New York, New York.

4 - Philip M. Stern, *The Best Congress Money Can Buy,* (New York, Pantheon Books, 1988), p.126

5 - *The Washington Report on Middle East Affairs,* July 1991, p.11.

6 - *Ibid,.* p.11.

7 - *Ibid.*, p.11.

8 - *Ibid.*, p.11.

9 - Findley, *op. cit.,* p.1.

10 - *Ibid.*, p.11.

11 - *Ibid.*, p.13.

12 - *Ibid.*, p.16.

13 - *Ibid.*, p.17.

14 - *Ibid.*, p.19.

15 - *Ibid.*, p.21.

16 - *Ibid.*, p.21.

17 - *Ibid.*, p.25.

18 - *Ibid.*, p.26.

19 - *Ibid.*, p.32.

20 - *Ibid.*, p.34.

21 - *Ibid.*, p.35.

22 - *Ibid.*, p.51.

23 - *Ibid.*, p.54.

24 - *Ibid.*, p.55.

25 - Curtiss, *op. cit.,* p.27.

26 - Findley, *op. cit.,* p.87.

27 - *Ibid.*, p.87.

28 - Findley *op. cit., p.* 88

29 - *Ibid.*, p.92.

30 - *Ibid.*, p.92.

31 - *Ibid.*, p.139-140.

32 - *Ibid.*, p.140.

33 - *Ibid.*, p.155.

34 - *Ibid.*, p.141.

35 - *Ibid.*, p.142-143.

36 - *Ibid.*, p.143.

37 - *Ibid.*, p.161.

38 - *Ibid.*, p.143. `

39 - Findley, *op. cit.*, p.180.

40 - *Ibid.*, p.181.

41 - *Ibid.*, p.182.

42 - *Ibid.*, p.183-184.

43 - *Ibid.*, p.191.

44 - *Ibid.*, p.192.

45 - *Ibid.*, p.192.

46 - *Ibid.*, p.195.

47 - *Ibid.*, p.214.

48 - *Ibid.*, p.213.

49 - *Ibid.*, p.223.

50 - *Ibid.*, p.248.

51 - *Ibid.*, p.253.

52 - *Ibid.*, p.258.

53- Grace Halsell, *Prophesy and Politics: Militant Evangelists on the Road to Nuclear War,* (Lawrence Hill and Company, Westport, Connecticut, 1986) p.74.

54 - Roselle Tekiner, Samir Abed-Rabbo, and Norton Mezvinshy, *Anti-Zionism: Analytical Reflections,* (Brattleboro, Vermont: Amana Books, 1989), p.261.

55 - Halsell, *op. cit.,* p.30-32.

56 - *Ibid.*, p.75.

57 - *Ibid.*, p.75.

58 - Teniner, Abed-Rabbo, Mezvinshy, *op. cit.,* p.259.

59 - Halsell, *op. cit.,* p.14.

60 - Teniner, Abed-Rabbo, Mezvinshy, *op. cit.,* p.260.

61 - Halsell, *op. cit.,* p.9.

62 - Teniner, Abed-Rabbo, Mezvinshy, *op. cit.,* p.260.

63 - Halsell, *op. cit.,* p.5.

64 - Leslie D. Weatherhead, *The Christian Agnostic,* (Nashville, Tennessee: Abingdon Press, 1965), p.95.

65 - Tehiner, Abed-Rabbo, Mezvinsky, *op. cit.,* 1989), p.201.

66 - Findley, *op. cit.,* p.117.

67 - *Ibid.*, p.118.
68 - *Ibid.*, p.119.
69 - *Ibid.*, p.119.
70 - *Ibid.*, p.21.
71 - *Ibid.*, p.80.
72 - *Ibid.*, p.126.
73 - *Ibid.*, p.126.
74 - James M. Ennes, Jr. *Assault on the Liberty*, (New York: Random House, 1979), p.210-211.
75 - Findley, *op. cit.*, p.167.
76 - *Ibid.*, p.167-168.
77 - *Ibid.*, p.168.
78 - *Ibid.*, p.168.
79 - David Lewis, Senior Research Office on board *Liberty*. Interviewed at the Twentieth Anniversary Memorial Service and Reunion, Washington, D.C. Video, *U.S.S. Liberty Survivors: Our Story*, (Sligo Productions, 1991)
80 - Narrator, Video, *U.S.S. Liberty Survivors: Our Story*, (Sligo Productions, 1991)
81 - James M. Ennes, Jr., Video, *U.S.S. Liberty Survivors: Our Story*, (Sligo Productions, 1991).
82 - Findley, *op. cit.*, p.169.
83 - *Ibid.*, p.171.
84 - *Ibid.*, p.179.
85 - Admiral Thomas Moorer, Interviewed at the Twentieth Anniversary Memorial Service and Reunion, Washington, D.C. Video, *U.S.S. Liberty Survivors: Our Story*, (Sligo Productions, 1991).

Chapter Seven - Justice and the Peace Process

1 - Elias Chacour, *Blood Brothers*, (Old Tappan, N.J: Chosen Books, Fleming H. Revell, 1984), p.118.
2 - Ralph Schoenman, *The Hidden History of Zionism*, (Santa Barbara, California: Veritas Press, 1988), p.29.
3 - Fred J. Khouri, *The Arab Israeli Dilema, Third Edition*, (Syracuse, N.Y.: Syracuse University Press, 1985), p.58.
4 - Alan Hart, *Arafat, Terrorist or Peacemaker*, (London: Sidgwick and Jackson, 1984), p.220.
5 - Paul Findley, *Deliberate Deceptions, Facing the Facts about the U.S.-Israeli Relationship*, (Chicago: Lawrence Hill Books, 1993), p.36.
6 - Clifford A. Wright, *Facts and Fables: The Arab-Israeli Conflict*. (New York: Kegan Paul International, 1989), p.132.
7 - Findley, *op. cit.*, p.36.
8 - Wright, *op. cit.*, p.132.
9 - Many believed Israel conspired a deal with Syria; no ground invasion

of Syria in exchange for only a face-saving token resistance in Golan Heights. This would enable Israel to concentrate forces against Egypt and gain a quick victory before world governments forced a cease fire. See Hart, pp 223-245.

10- *Ibid.*, p.96.

11- *Ibid.*, p.13

12- *U.S.A. Today,* January 21, 1991. Cited in *Breaking the Siege,* Volume 7, No. 6 February-March 1991, p.1.

13- Knowledge Products - Audio Cassette, *The World's Political Hotspots, The Middle East.* Wendy McElroy and Sheldon Richman. Narrated by Harry Reasoner. 1991.

14- Michael S. McManus, *Eloquent Sermons Ring Out on Lawn of the White House,* Intelligencer Journal, Lancaster, PA., Saturday, September 18, 1993, p.A-4.

15- Sami Hadawi, *Bitter Harvest, A Modern History of Palestine,* (New York: Olive Branch Press, 1989), p.189.

16- Wright, *op. cit.,* p.49. For a full list of Zionist 'firsts' see Walid Khalidi, "Towards an Adjustment of Political Perception in Arab Society," in Margaret Pennar,ed. *The Middle East: Five Perspectives,* Information paper 7, Aug, October 1973, p.14.

17- Nahum Barnea and Danny Rubenstein, *Davar,* March 19, 1982. Cited in Wright, p.49.

18- *Al Hamishmar,* March 3, 1978. Lt. Col. Dov. Yirmiah exposed the story of Lahis. See Noam Chomsky, *The Fateful Triangle: The United States, Israel, and the Palestinians,* Chapter 2. Cited in Wright., p.49.

19- Noam Chomsky, *op. cit.,* p. 165. Cited in Wright., p.49.

20- See Israel Shahak, *Begin and Co.: As They Really Are,* Jerusalem, 1977. Cited in Wright., p.49.

21- Colin Chapman, *Whose Promised Land,* (England: Lion International Paperback, 1983), p.92.

22- Hart, *op. cit.,* p.380.

23- Thomas L. Friedman, *From Beirut to Jerusalem,* (New York: Farrar Straus Giroux, 1988), p.130.

24- Hart, *op. cit.,* p.111.

25- *New York Times,* June 7, 1983. Cited in Hart., p.112.

26- Edward Said and Christopher Hitchens, *Blaming the Victims,* (New York: Verso, 1988), p.113.

27- *Ibid.*, p.113.

28- Hart, *op. cit.,* p. 450.

29- Said, *op. cit.,* p.115.

30- Thomas L. Friedman, *From Beirut to Jerusalem,* (New York: Farrar Straus Giroux, 1989), p.130.

31- George W. Ball and Douglas B. Ball, *The Passionate Attachment, America's Involvement with Israel, 1947 to the Present,* (New York: W.W. Norton, 1992), p.194.

32- Robert I. Friedman, *Zealots for Zion.* (New York: Random House, 1992), p.194.

33- Findley, *op. cit.,* p.154.

34- Editorial, "Fight Complacency on Human Rights Violations," *Breaking the Siege,* The Newsletter of the Middle East Justice Network, June-July, 1993, Vol 5, No.2, p.8

35- Eyad El-Sarraj, Director, Gaza Community Mental Health Program. *Mental Suffering Among Gazans on the Rise,* Al-Fajr, Feb. 22, 1993), p.5. Cited by James A Graff, "An Open Letter to Mrs. Clinton," *The Link,* Published by Americans for Middle East Understanding, New York, May-June, 1993, p.5.

36- *New York Times,* April 9, 1993. Cited in Editorial, "Rule by Gun and Roadblock Deepens Despair," *Breaking the Siege,* The Newsletter of the Middle East Justice Network, June- July 1993, Vol. 5 No.2.) p.1.

37- Daoud Kuttab, "In the Aftermath of the War," *Journal of Palestinian Studies.* #80, Volume XX, Number 4, Summer 1991, p.118.

38- Daniel Williams, "For Arafat's PLO, an Acceptance that "Times have Changed," *The Washington Post National Weekly Edition,* September 20-26, 1993, p.8.

39- Andrew Gowers and Tony Walker, *Behind the Myth, Yasser Arafat and the Palestinian Revolution,* (New York: Olive Branch Press, 1992), p.109.

40- *The Times* of London, November 16 and December 17, 1973. Cited in Gowers and Walker, *Arafat,* p.135.

41- PLO brochure distributed to press at Algiers Summit, June 1988. Cited in Gower and Walker, *Arafat,* p.284.

42- *New York Times,* December 15, 1988. Cited in Gower and Walker, *Arafat,* p.299.

43- Na'im Ateek, *Justice, and Only Justice,* (Maryknoll, New York: Orbis Books, 1989), p.164.

44- Editorial, "Beyond 'Good Will' Gestures: The Same Old Story, " *Breaking the Siege,* The Newsletter of the Middle East Justice Network, Oct-Nov. 1992, Vol.4, No.4, p.7

45- Geoffrey Aronson, "Mideast Win-Win," *Intelligencer Journal,* Lancaster, PA.,Sept. 21, 1993.

46- Sara Roy, "What Next for Gaza?" *The Christian Sceince Monitor,* Monday, September 13, 1993.

47- David R. Francis, "Economic Issues Are Key to Mideast Peace," *Christian Science Monitor,* Friday, September 17, 1993.

48- Frank Collins, "Palestinian Economy in Chaos After Gulf War," *The Washington Report on Middle East Affairs.* July 1991,Volume X, Number 2, p.23.

49- The Database Project on Palestine Human Rights, *The Cost of Freedom.* 1988 A Special Report , p.48.

50- Ben Lynfield, "Israel Looks Abroad To Fund Peace Pact, " *The Christian Science Monitor,* Friday, September 17, 1993.

51- Findley, *op. cit.,* p.120.

52- Israel Shahak, "Why Israel Can Never Repay the Loans to be Guaranteed by the US," *The Washington Report on Middle East Affairs.* November 1991, Vol. X. No.5,,p.18.

53- Findley, *op. cit.,* p.117.

54- *Ibid.,* p.118.

Chapter Eight - What Christians Can Do

1 - Robert McAfee Brown, *Unexpected News, Reading the Bible with Third World Eyes,* (Philidelphia: Westminster Press, 1984), p.137

2 - Lauree Hersch Meyer and Melanie A. May, *Palestinians and the Power of Hope, The Christian Century,* Vol. 109, No.6, February 19, 1992, p.180-181.

3 - See: Al Haq Annual Report on Human Rights, 1989, *A Nation Under Siege* , p.525-525. Also see *The Right to Unite,* Occasional Paper No.8, Al Haq, and Rizeq Shuqair and Randa Siniora, *Application Denied,* Prepared by Al Haq.

4 - Personal interview, Ramallah, July 8, 1991

5 - Personal Conversation, Jerusalem, July 9, 1991

6 - Donald E. Wagner, "Holy Land Christians Worry about Survival," *The Christian Century,* p.452

7 - *Ibid.,* p.452.

8 - Personal Conversation, Ibillin, July 7, 1991

BIBLIOGRAPHY

Affirmation - Union Theological Seminary, Richmond, Virginia, Spring 1990 - *Middle East Perspectives.*

Al-Haq Annual Report on Human Rights in the Occupied Territories, *A Nation Under Siege,* Al Haq, Ramallah, West Bank, 1989.

Amnesty International Report, 1991, New York: Amnesty International, 1991.

Aburish, Said K. *Cry Palestine, Inside the West Bank.* Boulder: Westview Press, 1993.

Alexander, Tonah and Sinai, Joshua. *Terrorism: The PLO Connection.* New York: Crane Russsak, 1989.

Ang, Swee Chai. *From Beirut to Jerusalem.* London: Grafton Books, 1989.

Arias, Esther and Mortimer. *The Cry of My People.* New York: Friendship Press, 1980.

Ateek, Na'im. *Justice and Only Justice.* Maryknoll: Orbis Books, 1989.

Avallone, Michael. *A Woman Called Golda.* New York: Leisure Books, 1982.

Baker, Ross. *The New Fat Cats, Members of Congress as Political Benefactors.* New York: Priority Press, 1989.

Ball, George W. and Douglas B. *The Passionate Attatchment.* New York: W.W. Norton, 1992.

Bennis, Phillis and Michel Moushabeck. *Beyond the Storm.* New York: Olive Branch Press, 1991.

Benziman, Uzi. *Sharon, An Israeli Caesar.* New York: Adama Books, 1985.

Bergan, Kathy, David Neuhaus, and Ghassan Rubeiz, Editors. *Justice and the Intifada, Palestinians and Israelis Speak Out.* New York: Friendship Press, 1991.

Berryman, Phillip. *Liberation Theology.* New York: Pantheon Books, 1987.

Brown, Robert McAfee. *Making Peace in the Global Village.* Louisville, KY.: Westminster/John Knox, 1981.

_____ *Religion and Violence.* Louisville, KY.: Westminster/John Knox, 1987.

_____ *Saying Yes and Saying No, On Rendering to God and Caesar.* Louisville, KY.: Westminster/John Knox, 1986.

_____ *Spirituality and Liberation, Overcoming the Great Fallacy.* Louisville, KY.: Westminster/John Knox, 1988.

_____ *Unexpected News, Reading the Bible with Third World Eyes.* Louisville, KY.: Westminster/John Knox, 1984.

189

BIBLIOGRAPHY

Brown, William R. *The Last Crusade, A Negotiator's Middle East Handbook.* Chicago: Nelson-Hall, 1980.

Carter, Jimmy. *The Blood of Abraham.* Boston: Houghton, 1985.

_____ *Keeping Faith, Memoirs of a President.* New York: Bantam Books, 1982.

Cassese, Antonio. *Terrorism, Politics and Law, The Achille Lauro Affair.* Princeton: Princeton University Press, 1989.

Chacour, Elias. *Blood Brothers.* Old Tappan, N.J.: Fleming H. Revell, 1984.

_____ *We Belong to the Land.* San Fransisco, Harper, 1990.

Chapman, Colin. *Whose Promised Land.* Batavia, Illinois: Lion Publishing, 1983.

Chomsky, Noam. *The Fateful Triangle, The United States, Israel, and the Palestinians.* Boston: South End Press, 1983.

_____ *Pirates and Emperors, International Terrorism in the Real World.* Brattleboro, Vermont: Amana Books, 1990.

Collins, Larry and Dominique Lapierre. *O Jerusalem.* New York: Simon and Schuster, 1972.

Cone, James H. *God of the Oppressed.* San Francisco: Harper and Row, 1975, pp.280

Cooley, John K. *Payback, America's Long War in the Middle East.* Washington: Brassey, Inc., 1991.

Cuddihy, John Murray. *No Offense, Civil Religion and Protestant Taste.* New York: Crossroad Book, 1978.

Curtiss, Richard H. *A Changing Image, American Perceptions of the Arab-Israeli Dispute.* Washington, D.C.: American Education Trust, 1986.

_____ *Stealth PACs, How Israel's American Lobby Seeks to Control U.S. Middle East Policy.* Washington, D.C.: American Education Trust, 1990.

The DataBase Project of Palestinian Human Rights, *The Cost of Freedom.* Palestinian Human Rights under Israeli Occupation, 1988.

Dillman, Jeffrey D. and Musa A. Bakri. *Israel's Use of Electric Shock Torture in the Interrogation of Palestinian Detainees.* Chicago: Palestinian Human Rights Information Center, 1991.

Dobson, Christopher and Ronald Payne, *The Never Ending War.* New York: Facts on File, 1987.

Dunn, Charles W. *Religion in American Politics.* Washington, D.C.: Clemson University Press, A Division of Washington Quarterly, 1989.

Ellis, Marc H. *Beyond Innocence and Redemption.* New York: Harper and Row, 1990.

_____ *Toward a Jewish Theology of Liberation.* Maryknoll, NY.: Orbis Books, 1987.

_____ and Rosemary Ruether. *Beyond Occupation.* Boston: Beacon Press, 1990.

Emmerson, Gloria. *Gaza, A Year in the Intifada.* New York: Atlantic Monthly Press, 1991.

Ennes, Jr., James M. *Assault on the Liberty.* New York: Random House, 1979.

Feuerlicht, Roberta. *The Fate of the Jews.* New York: Times Books, 1983.

Findley, Paul. *They Dare to Speak Out.* Westport, Connecticut: Lawrence Hill, 1985.

_____ *Deliberate Deceptions.* Chicago: Lawrence Hill, 1993.

Flapin, Simha. *The Birth of Israel.* New York: Pantheon Books, 1987.

Friedman, Thomas L. *From Beirut to Jerusalem.* New York: Farrar, Straus Giroux, 1989.

Gilpin, W. Clark, Editor. *Public Faith, Reflections on the Political Role of American Churches.* St. Louis, Missouri: CBP Press, 1990.

Grossman, David. *Sleeping on a Wire, Conversations with Palestinians in Israel.* New York: Farrar Straus and Giroux, 1993.

Graham-Brown, Sarah. *The Palestinian Situation.* Geneva, Switzerland: World Alliance of Young Men's Christian Association, 1989.

Green, Stephen. *Taking Sides, America's Secret Relations with a Militant Israel,* Brattleboro, Vermont: Amana Books, 1988.

Gutierrez, Gustavo. *A Theology of Liberation.* Maryknoll, NY.: Orbis Books, 1973.

Hadawi, Sami. *Bitter Harvest, A Modern History of Palestine.* New York: Olive Branch Press, 1989.

Haddad, Hassan and Donald Wagner. *All in the Name of the Bible,* Brattleboro, Vermont: Amana Books, 1986.

Haines, Byron L. and Frank L. Cooley, Editors. *Christians and Muslims Together.* Philadelphia: Geneva Press, 1987.

Halsell, Grace. *Journey to Jerusalem.* New York: Macmillan Publishing, 1981.

_____ *Prophesy and Politics.* Chicago: Lawrence Hill, 1986.

Harkabi, Yehoshafat. *Israel's Fateful Hour.* New York: Harper and Row, 1986.

Hart, Alan. *Arafat, Terrorist or Peacemaker.* London: Sidgwick and Jackson, 1984.

Hourani, Albert. *A History of the Arab Peoples.* Cambridge, Mass.: Belknap Press, 1991.

Hurwitz, Deena. *Walking the Red Line.* Philadelphia: New Society Publishers, 1992.

Hutcheson, Richard G. *God in the White House.* New York: MacMillan Company, 1988.

Khavari, Farid A. *Oil and Islam, The Ticking Bomb.* Malibu, CA.: Roundtable Publishing, 1990.

Khouri, Fred J. *The Arab-Israeli Dilemma.* Syracuse, N.Y.: Third Edition, Syracuse University Press, 1985.

Kimball, Charles A. *Angle of Vision, Christians and the Middle East.* New York: Friendship Press, 1992.

BIBLIOGRAPHY

Lamb, David. *The Arabs, Journeys Beyond the Mirage.* New York: Vintage Books, 1987.

Laqueur, Walter and Yonah Alexander. *The Terrorism Reader.* New York: New American Library, 1987.

Lindsey, Hal. *The Late Great Planet Earth.* New York: Bantam Books, 1970.

Livingstone, Neil C. and David Halevy. *Inside the PLO.* New York: Quill/ Williams Morrow, 1990.

Long, David E. *The Anatomy of Terrorism.* New York: MacMillian International, 1990.

Mackey, Sandra. *Lebanon, Death of a Nation.* New York: Congdon and Weed, 1989.

Mansfield, Peter. *A History of the Middle East.* New York: Viking, 1991.

Mayhew, Peter. *A Theology of Force and Violence.* Philadelphia: Trinity Press, 1989.

McDowell, David. *Palestine and Israel, The Uprising and Beyond.* Berkeley, Los Angeles: University of California Press, 1989.

Mendelsohn, Everett. *A Compassionate Peace.* A Report Prepared for the American Friends Service Committee, New York: Farrar, Straus, and Giroux, 1989.

Nakhleh, Issa. *Encylocpedia of the Palestinian Problem.* New York: Intercontinental Books, Vol.1 & 2, 1991.

Noll, Mark A. *One Nation Under God.* San Francisco: Harper and Row, 1988.

Ostrovsky, Victor and Clair Hoy. *By Way of Deception.* New York: St. Martin's Press, 1990.

Pearson, Anthony. *Conspiracy of Silence.* London: Quartet Books, 1978.

Pippert, Wesley G. *Land of Promise, Land of Strife.* Waco, Texas: Word Books, 1988.

Ramsey, William M. *The Wall of Separation.* Louisville, KY.: Westminster/John Knox, 1989.

Reich, Walter. *Origins of Terrorism.* New York: Cambridge University Press, 1990.

Robertson, Edwin. *The Shame and The Sacrifice, The Life and Martyrdom of Dietrich Bonhoeffer.* New York: Macmillian and Company, 1988.

Rokach, Livia. *Israel's Sacred Terrorism, A Study based on Moshe Sharett's Personal Diary.* Association of Arab-American University Graduates, 1986.

Rubinstein, Danny. *The People of Nowhere,* New York: Times Books, 1991.

Sallinger, Pierre. *Secret Dossier, The Hidden Agenda behind the Gulf War,* New York: Penguin Books, 1991.

Said, Edward and Christopher Hitchens. *Blaming the Victims.* New York: Verso, 1988.

_____ *The Question of Palestine*. New York: Vintage Press, 1992.

Schiff, Ze'ev and Ehud Ya'ari. *Intifada*. New York: Simon and Schuster, 1990.

Schoenman, Ralph. *The Hidden History of Zionism*. Santa Barbara, Calif.: Veritas Press, 1988.

Segal, Jerome M. *Creating the Palestinian State, A Strategy for Peace*. Chicago: Lawrence Hill Books. 1989.

Segav, Tom. *1949, The First Israeli*. New York: Macmillan, 1986.

Shaheen, Jack G. *The T.V. Arab*. Bowling Green, Ohio: Bowling Green University Press, 1984.

Sharon, Ariel. *Warrior, An Autobiography*. New York: Touchstone Book (Simon and Schuster), 1989.

Shipler, David K. *Arab and Jew, Wounded Spirits in a Promised Land*. New York: Penguin Books, 1986.

Simon, Arthur. *Christian Faith and Public Policy, No Grounds for Divorce*. Grand Rapids, Michigan: Eerdmans, 1987.

Spong, John Shelby. *This Hebrew Lord*. San Francisco: Harper and Row, 1988.

Stern, Philip M. *The Best Congress Money Can Buy*. New York: Pantheon Books, 1988.

Stone, Ronald H. *Christian Realism and Peace-Making, Issues in U.S. Foreign Policy*. Nashville: Abingdon Press, 1988.

_____ Editor. *Reformed Faith and Politics*. Washington, D.C.: University Press of America, 1983.

Tekiner, Roselle, Samir Abed-Rabbo and Norton Mezvinsky, *Anti-Zionism*. Brattleboro, Vermont: Amana Books, 1989.

Timerman, Jacobo. *The Longest War, Israel in Lebanon*. New York: Alfred A. Knopf, 1982.

_____ *Prisoner without a Name, Cell without a Number*. New York: Vintage Books, 1881.

Tivnan, Edward. *The Lobby, Jewish Political Power and American Foreign Policy*. New York: Touchstone Book, 1987.

Wall, James M. *Winning the War, Losing Our Souls*. Chicago: Christian Century Press, 1991.

Wallach, Janet and John. *Arafat, in the Eye of the Beholder*. New York: Carol Publishing Group, 1990.

_____ *The New Palestinians, The Emerging Generation of Leaders*. Rocklin, CA.: Prima Publishers, 1992.

Weinberg, Leonard B. and Paul B. Davis. *Introduction to Political Terrorism*. New York: McGraw-Hill Publishing Company, 1989.

Wright, Clifford A. *Facts and Fables: The Arab -Israeli Conflict*. New York: Kegan Paul International, 1989.

Weinstick, Nathan. *Zionism: False Messiah*. London: Pluto Press, 1969.

Weir, Ben and Carol. *Hostage Bound, Hostage Free*. Louisville, KY.: Westminster/ John Knox, 1987.

BIBLIOGRAPHY

SPECIAL RESOURCES

Journal Graphics, Inc. 1991 Transcript/Video Index, Television News & Public Affairs Programming, (Annual)
1535 Grant Street
Denver, CO. 80203

The Almanac of American Politics, 1991, The Senators, the Representatives and the Governors: Their records and Election results, Their State and Districts, Michael Barone and Grant Ujifusa, (Annual)
National Journal,
LB 8621
P.O. Box 7247
Philadelphia, PA. 19101-9654

Journal of Palestinian Studies, A Quarterly on Palestinian Affairs and the Arab-Israeli Conflict, Published by The Institute for Palestinian Studies,
University of California Press,
P.O. Box 25301
Georgetown Station
Washington, D.C. 20007

194